Leading the Way

Amy Morris Homans in 1889

Leading the Way

AMY MORRIS HOMANS AND THE BEGINNINGS OF PROFESSIONAL EDUCATION FOR WOMEN

Betty Spears

CONTRIBUTIONS IN WOMEN'S STUDIES,
NUMBER 64

 GREENWOOD PRESS

NEW YORK
WESTPORT, CONNECTICUT
LONDON

Library of Congress Cataloging-in-Publication Data

Spears, Betty.
  Leading the way.

  (Contributions in women's studies, ISSN 0147-104X ;
no. 64)
    Bibliography: p.
    Includes index.
    1. Physical education for women—United States—
History. 2. Homans, Amy Morris, d. 1933. 3. Educators—
United States—Biography. 4. Professional education
of women—United States—History. I. Title. II. Series.
GV439.S64   1986   613.7′045′0924 [B]   85-21872
ISBN 0-313-25107-X (lib. bdg. : alk. paper)

Library of Congress Catalog Card Number: 85-21872
ISBN: 0-313-25107-X
ISSN: 0147-104X

First published in 1986

Greenwood Press, Inc.
88 Post Road West
Westport, Connecticut 06881

Printed in the United States of America

The paper used in this book complies with the
Permanent Paper Standard issued by the National
Information Standards Organization (Z39.48-1984).

10 9 8 7 6 5 4 3 2 1

Copyright Acknowledgment

Grateful acknowledgment is given to the following: Hampton
University Archives, Hampton, VA; Winthrop College, Archives
and Special Collections, Rock Hill, SC; Minutes of the Corporation of Simmons College, The Colonel Miriam E. Perry Goll Archives, Simmons College, Boston, MA; Peabody Museum, Salem,
MA; Wellesley College Archives, Wellesley, MA. All illustrations
courtesy of the Wellesley College Archives, used with permission.

To the generations yet unborn
so that they may know and
understand their heritage

Contents

Illustrations

Acknowledgments

Many colleagues, archivists, librarians, and friends encouraged and assisted me in the preparation of this work. First, however, I wish to express my appreciation to Helen Hazelton '19, director of physical education for women at Purdue University, for her role in this project. During my senior year at Purdue, she suggested that I apply to Wellesley College for graduate study in physical education. At Wellesley, I was introduced to a professional world where women were expected to be competent, independent, and successful. Gradually, I came to understand that these expectancies were part of the Amy Morris Homans tradition. I owe Miss Hazelton a debt of gratitude for starting me on a course of action that led to this book.

In 1960, seven years after the termination of the graduate program in hygiene and physical education at Wellesley, I returned as director of physical education. While answering inquiries about the Boston Normal School of Gymnastics, the professional programs of the department, and Amy Morris Homans I collected a considerable amount of data. During a leave in 1967-1968 at the University of Southern California, Aileene Lockhart and Eleanor Metheny encouraged me to investigate Homans' role in the development of physical education. That research led to the wider topic of the beginnings of professional education for women.

I am grateful to the many librarians and archivists who delved into records, rummaged in closets and attics, and searched for much-needed evidence. In the last years of this research, the records and memorabilia of the Department of Physical Education and the Edith Hemenway Eustis Library in Mary Hemenway Hall at Wellesley were relocated in the Wellesley College Archives. Wilma Slaight, the Wellesley College Archivist, rendered valuable assistance in locating important Wellesley College and Boston Normal School of Gymnastics documents and in making needed changes in citations. Elaine Smith's discussions greatly benefited this work and Julia Demmin asked the right questions at the right time. Finally, I wish to acknowledge and express my appreciation for the support of many personal and professional friends who have cheerfully and patiently followed this project to its completion.

Leading the Way

1

Prologue

Amy Morris Homans' remarkable career in the education of women began in 1889 when she became the director of the Boston Normal School of Gymnastics (BNSG) and ended in the 1920s, well after she had retired as professor emeritus from Wellesley College. At a time when many physicians and other authorities still questioned exercise and higher education for women, Homans and her employer and friend, Mrs. Mary Hemenway, joined the social reformers who believed that exercise could better the lives of children and, therefore, future generations. Seeking to improve the health and vigor of Boston's girls and boys, these two women persuaded the Boston School Committee to require Swedish gymnastics in the public schools. To supply gymnastics teachers, Hemenway established the Boston Normal School of Gymnastics and named Homans the director. Then 40 years old and an experienced teacher and administrator, Homans saw beyond the immediate, local situation in Boston and envisioned, pursued, and achieved a profession of physical education for women.

Beginning with a two-year normal school and two faculty members in Boston, twenty years later Homans became the director of the Department of Hygiene and Physical Education at Wellesley College. At Wellesley, with fourteen faculty and staff members, she conducted an undergraduate program of exercise, sport, and dance, and initiated a graduate program in physical education. At a time when few women held faculty or administrative appointments in higher education, she educated her students to assume such positions, instilling in them a rare combination of executive skills and professional dedication. Homans demanded excellence both in and out of the classroom. In addition to their academic courses, the students learned social graces, professional etiquette, and "womanliness." For Homans, "womanliness" did not imply a passive, submissive, wan woman, but a healthy, vigorous, competent woman with flawless manners who was faultlessly dressed and immaculately groomed. Insisting on perfection, she summarily dismissed students who did not meet these standards. Many of those who survived became administrators and leaders in the emerging profession of physical education for women. By the 1920s, scores of BNSG/Wellesley alumnae directed programs of physical education across the United States and in several foreign countries.

In spite of the growing number of women who attended college and worked outside the home in the late-nineteenth century, the beliefs persisted that women were physically and mentally inferior to men, that they belonged in the home, and that they could not and should not undertake administrative and leadership positions in the professional world. Many social reformers of the period approved the growing interest in exercise as a means of increasing the general health of the citizenry and also promoted robust, outdoor sport for men to increase their virility. However, some of these same reformers and the public at large decried strenuous exercise and sport as improper and unfeminine for women. Through her unique approach to education, Homans demonstrated that women could attain health and vigor through exercise and sport without losing their femininity, could undertake advanced study, and could hold leadership positions.

In the perspective of today's study of professions, Homans' actions are the more remarkable. While contemporary scholars characterize a profession in a variety of ways, four criteria consistently appear in the literature. First, a profession must focus on humanitarian and community concerns rather than on business or profit matters. Second, a profession adopts philosophic positions to guide its conduct and development. Third, members of a profession engage in study and research to further knowledge in the discipline or field; and fourth, a profession establishes qualifications, defines appropriate attitudes and behaviors, and promotes a sense of community among its members.[1]

Under Homans' masterful and indefatigable leadership, physical education for women fulfilled these criteria. To succeed, a profession requires leaders, and Homans carefully selected her students and educated them to meet this special demand. First at BNSG and later at Wellesley, Homans subjected her students to a special blend of extraordinarily rigorous academic, physical, social, and personal experiences, from which they emerged well prepared to accept leadership positions.

With its emphasis on preparing women for administrative positions, the education to which Homans subjected her students marked a departure from the professional education available to most women of the late-nineteenth century. Of the few women who did enter the professions at that time, most became elementary school teachers, nurses, and librarians. Some became artists and art teachers, authors, and secondary school teachers, while a very few became college teachers, physicians, lawyers, and engineers.[2] Preparation for these careers varied widely. Teacher education depended, to a large extent, on the standards of the local community or of the founders of proprietary schools in subjects such as art and business.

Some women who became elementary school teachers completed their education at an academy and continued to read, travel, and educate themselves. Others attended normal schools, some of which offered college level courses, and those who enrolled in proprietary schools studied the specialty of the institution and related subjects.[3]

Nurses were trained in schools connected with hospitals which offered some lectures and a practical apprenticeship. In 1880 there were fifteen nurses' training schools with 323 pupils and 157 graduates.[4] The first professional library course, approved by the trustees of Columbia College in 1884, did not begin until 1887. The library students enrolled in a three-month practical training combined with two years of work experience, completing their program with a three-month review.[5] Admission to medical and legal studies did not yet require a college degree.

Colleges such as Mount Holyoke, Vassar, Wellesley, and Smith offered a liberal arts education but, with the exception of teaching, did not concern themselves with education for the professions. In this atmosphere, with little professional education for women in existence, and higher education for women emerging from its shaky beginnings, Homans created her programs based on her own teaching experiences, observations, and vision of the future. She patterned her professional education programs after Boston's liberal arts colleges and universities and the Royal Central Institute of Gymnastics in Sweden.

Described as a reserved, well-mannered, indomitable New England lady, Amy Morris Homans did not want her biography written. A few months before her death in 1933, Homans refused permission to Marion Watters Babcock '10, her former student and then confidant, to begin her biography. Homans told her, "If what I have done is worth anything, it will live. If it is of no use, let it die with me."[6] At her request, Eugene Howe, a loyal faculty member of Wellesley College, Agnes Dodge, a Wellesley librarian, and Gertrude, Homans' sister, destroyed most of her papers and correspondence. How much first-hand information about her life was discarded is unknown, for these three are no longer living.

A few years after Homans' death, efforts were made to collect and record information about her career. In 1936, Howe and other senior members of Wellesley's Department of Hygiene and Physical Education prepared an unpublished statement of Homans' principles and policies which played a significant role in her success.[7] During the late 1930s and early 1940s Howe, in collaboration with Elmo A. Robinson, Howe's assistant at Wellesley in 1913–1914 and a close friend, corresponded with a number of BNSG/Wellesley alumnae to obtain information about Homans' "educational philosophy and her relationship to other educational movements and leaders of her time."[8] Robinson abandoned the project after Howe's death and, in 1953, sent a thirteen page compilation of data and pertinent correspondence to Margaret Clapp, president of Wellesley College. In 1938 Margery Taylor '39 compiled a wealth of material on the professional training at BNSG and Wellesley[9] and, in 1941, William Skarstrom '95 prepared Homans' sketch which appeared in the *Supplement to the Research Quarterly, Pioneer Women in Physical Education.*[10]

Skarstrom's brief biography, written as a former student and loyal faculty member, is an admirable sketch of Homans and appropriately places her in the vanguard of women physical educators. Written in 1941, it understandably does not treat Homans' contributions to the professional education of women. In the context of today's increasing in-depth study of women, their education, and their entry into professions, Homans' story assumes added significance.

As Homans wished, this work is not a biography. Instead, it is the story of Homans' struggles to gain the acceptance of physical education as a profession for women and her unique approach to educating women to be leaders in that profession. The search for information about Homans revealed more than originally thought possible. At Wellesley College, the Edith Hemenway Eustis Library in Mary Hemenway Hall, the alumnae *Bulletin*, department and college records, and other memorabilia contained rewarding material.[11] Additional information has been found in many libraries and private collections in the Boston area; in Vassalboro, Maine, where Homans spent her girlhood; and in Wilmington, North Carolina, where she taught with her aunt, Amy Morris Bradley, and met Hemenway, her employer and the founder of BNSG. From Maine to California, more than 40 alumnae from the classes of 1899 to 1926 have been interviewed. Their recollections, diaries, and encouragement have been invaluable.

BNSG was not the first institution to train physical education teachers. In 1881 Dudley A. Sargent, director of the Hemenway Gymnasium at Harvard University, opened a normal school to train women physical education teachers. By 1885 the American-German Turners had established the Normal School of the North American Gymnastic Union in Milwaukee, Wisconsin and, a year later, William G. Anderson founded the Brooklyn Normal School. Both were open to men and women. In 1887 the Young Men's Christian Association School in Springfield, Massachusetts, initiated a program to train men gymnasium directors.

Nor was Homans the only woman pioneer in physical education. Typical of other new fields, most of the early leaders were men, but several women made significant contributions to the beginnings of physical education and, particularly, physical education for women. The 1941 monograph, *Pioneer Women in Physical Education* recognized "those early pioneers whose names and activities are best known."[12] The first biography is that of Amy Morris Homans, followed by twelve others. Eliza Marie Mosher and Clelia Duel Mosher, both physicians but not related, collected accurate data on women's physiology, helping to dispel superstitions and myths surrounding menstruation and other normal female functions. Delphine Hanna, also a physician, taught at Oberlin College from 1885 to 1920. In her long tenure at Oberlin she trained many future physical education leaders and also published anthropometric information on women. Other pioneers instituted prototype physical education programs at Vassar College, Smith College, Stanford University, New York City public schools, and the Detroit schools. Senda Berenson '92 is credited with adapting basketball for women and Constance M. K. Applebee with introducing and promoting field hockey. Of the thirteen pioneer women included in the monograph, three—Senda Berenson '92, Ethel Perrin '92, and Lillian Curtis Drew '93—are graduates of BNSG. In addition to her pioneering efforts in basketball, Berenson directed physical education at Smith College. Perrin taught at BNSG and later instituted Detroit's well-known public school physical education program. Drew, who specialized in corrective gymnastics, taught at Columbia University and at the Central School of Hygiene and Physical Education in New York, founded by another BNSG alumna, Helen McKinstry '00.[13]

While all these women made significant contributions to the slowly changing attitudes toward women, women's sport, and women's education, only Homans envisioned physical education as a profession for women. Under her leadership, women physical educators sought to improve the health of the citizenry, to advance knowledge in physical education, to adopt a code of conduct for members of the profession, to form a national society to promote a community of women physical educators, and to develop a *profession*. Set against the social and economic forces affecting women of the period and the beginnings of physical education, Homans' achievements were most remarkable. The story of how she educated women for new roles in a changing society adds to our understanding of the history of women's education, the history of exercise and sport for women, and the beginnings of professional education for women.

2

From Country School Teacher to Boston Reformer

Amy Morris Homans spent her childhood near Vassalboro, Maine, one of the many small, attractive towns northeast of Augusta along the Kennebec River. Settled in the mid-eighteenth century by hardy farmers, many of whom were also staunch Quakers, the town thrived in the decades prior to the Civil War. The Homans and the Bradleys, both Yankee families of long standing, moved to the area sometime before 1837, the year that Sarah Bradley married Harrison Homans. Listed in the local census as a farmer, Harrison Homans owned a number of parcels of land and provided comfortably for his family of five children. Amy Morris Homans was the third of these children. Clara was born in 1837, George in 1845, Amy Morris on November 15, 1848, Emma in 1854, and Gertrude in 1856.

Morris, as the family called Amy Morris Homans, grew up in an extended household consisting of her parents, her brother and sisters, her brother-in-law Benjamin Whitehouse, Grandfather Bradley, and, at times, Aunt Amy Morris Bradley. Morris attended Vassalboro Academy briefly and, perhaps, was instructed privately in history, literature, and languages.[1] Like many other young women who had mastered the basic school subjects, Morris began to teach in the local schools. Her first evaluation, made in 1865 by the town supervising committee, attests to her ability, her seriousness, and her success. "We have never witnessed a more successful effort on the part of a teacher who had not had experience before, than was shown by this instructress. The order, one of the most important requisites in the schoolroom, was excellent. Improvement good."[2] Homans expected her students to learn and did not permit confusion and disorder. She set about her tasks with "energy and determination," qualities which characterized her throughout her life.

Morris and her younger sister, Gertrude or Trudy, entered the nearby Quaker academy, Oak Grove Seminary, in the fall of 1867. The curriculum included a thorough study of English with special attention to students, usually boys, preparing for college. The school stressed high moral standards and expected the students to attend meeting on First-day or Sunday. Amy Morris Homans was graduated from Oak Grove in 1868 and the following year remained at the school as an assistant. Homans' formal education was over. The young men who were graduated from Oak Grove might attend a nearby college or leave Maine for further education but, because little higher education for women existed in the 1860s, the young women graduates did not have these same opportunities. Colleges which women might attend such as Oberlin in Ohio and Vassar in New York were a great distance from Maine. Even Mount Holyoke in Massachusetts may have seemed too far. We do not know whether these colleges may have been too costly or if the Homanses considered educating their daughters beyond Oak Grove. It is logical to assume that the family felt that they had done well to provide some formal education for two of their girls. Homans had not married by the time she was nineteen and her parents may have been grateful that her education had prepared her for teaching, one of the few careers available to women in the 1860s.

In the fall of 1869, Homans left Maine to teach with her aunt, Amy Morris Bradley, in Wilmington, North Carolina, joining the more than 5,000 Yankee school teachers who flooded the South after the Civil War. Many Southern communities, their educational funds depleted by the war, could not reopen their schools and were forced to accept aid from Northern philanthropic associations and teachers. Some of the teachers were employed by these associations, while others went south voluntarily to assist in the Reconstruction efforts. Still others, in their own way, sought to atone for some of the misery the North had inflicted on the South.[3]

Two philanthropic associations, the Unitarian Association and the Soldiers' Memorial Society of Boston, sponsored a school in Wilmington and appointed Bradley to conduct it. When Bradley arrived in Wilmington in January, 1867, she began the project alone in the Union Grammar School, but soon required two assistants. In 1868, with the help of local citizens, the Freedmen's Bureau, the Peabody Fund, and a wealthy Boston philanthropist, Mrs. Mary Hemenway, Bradley expanded the project to two schools, the Union and the Hemenway, named in honor of Mrs. Hemenway. A third school, the Pioneer, opened in January, 1869.[4] We do not know if Homans had any motivation in going to North Carolina other than earning a living, but we do know that the move was a turning point in her career and, unlike most single women of the times, she never returned to make her home with her parents.

In Wilmington she joined Bradley in instituting educational practices far ahead of their day, became an administrator at a very young age, and met her future employer and benefactor, Mrs. Mary Hemenway. She also faced skepticism and social ostracism from some Southerners. While many local residents supported the efforts of the Northern philanthropists, others regarded the "Yankee teachers" as outsiders. Not only were Northerners offering education which the Southerners could not afford to provide, but some of the Northern-sponsored schools were supported by Unitarians, subjects of deep suspicion from the traditional Southern trinitarians. In Wilmington a local newspaper "warned the people against this attempt 'by the societies of New England professing the doctrines of Free-Love-ism, Communism, Universalism, Unitarianism, and all the multiplicity of evil teachings that corrupt society and overthrow religion.' "[5] At one time a problem arose when the teachers could not find suitable living quarters. Finally, the mayor of Wilmington, Silas N. Martin, made arrangements for Bradley and her teachers.[6] In another instance, Bradley had been led to believe that she would be named County Examiner of the Schools, but the decision seemed to be unnecessarily delayed. Bradley considered closing the Wilmington schools because of such difficulties, but finally local authorities intervened and the schools continued.

By 1872 Bradley believed that a normal school[7] would increase the educational opportunities in Wilmington and appealed to Hemenway, who responded in characteristic fashion by donating $30,000.00 to construct the school and guaranteeing $5,000.00 each year for twenty years to support it. Bradley appointed Homans the principal of the new school. Homans introduced many innovative educational ideas, such as improving the students' writing abilities by publishing a school newspaper and sponsoring a literary club. The newspaper, *The Lighthouse*, contained articles written by the students, reprints from other publications, and short proverbs emphasizing the rewards of right living and right thinking. Knowing that most of the normal school students would not attend college, Homans and Bradley prepared them for practical jobs as tradesmen, carpenters, masons and blacksmiths, to name a few.

During her years in Wilmington, first as a young teacher, then as a principal of an elementary school, and, finally, as an administrator of a normal school, Homans grew into a competent executive with unusual administrative abilities and high personal standards. Sometime in these years between 1869 and 1876, perhaps during Hemenway's visits to Wilmington, Homans became acquainted with her future employer. As we have no record of conversations, letters, or interviews between the two women, we may assume that Hemenway came to know Homans and her work during these visits.[8] Hemenway, beginning to expand her philanthropic ventures, may have needed an assistant or, perhaps, she saw the makings of a capable administrator in Homans. Either reason would have been consistent with Hemenway's conduct of her affairs. Recently widowed, she lived in Boston with her children on fashionable Mt. Vernon Street and had, following the Civil War, become increasingly active in Boston's social reforms.

When Homans went north to work for Hemenway in 1876, she entered into a life which contrasted sharply with that in Wilmington. Bostonians considered their city the cultural hub of the United States. They prided themselves on Bulfinch's State House architecture, Frederick Law Olmstead's landscaping, and the many fine sculptures in the parks and public spaces. They enjoyed the writings of authors such as Richard Henry Dana,

Oliver Wendell Holmes, Julia Ward Howe, and Edward Everett Hale. The Boston Symphony Orchestra, founded in 1881, and the long-established Handel and Haydn Society furnished the city with good music. The citizens boasted of their educational institutions—Harvard College, Tufts College, the Massachusetts Institute of Technology, Boston College, Boston University, and others such as nearby Wellesley College for women.[9]

Like other Atlantic seaboard cities of the late-nineteenth century, Boston became the home of thousands of immigrants seeking a better life in the United States. These newcomers changed the ethnic mixture of Boston but not the fundamental character of the city. In 1880 Boston's population numbered 362,829, about 60 percent of whom considered themselves colonial Americans, English-speaking Canadians, Newfoundlanders, or other British stock. Italian and Jewish immigrants accounted for about 20 to 25 percent and 10 percent came from northern Europe, with the remaining small percentage scattered among Europeans from other countries, blacks, and Chinese.[10] Although the immigrants faced language barriers, strange customs, new laws, and difficulties in finding work, at the same time they took great pride in their new homeland and their new city. In a survey of Boston's population, William A. Leahy found that:

Life in Boston has its constant aspects. . . . Many of the newcomers think and feel very much as the older citizens do. For one thing, the colonial stock and what may be called its natural allies are . . . stronger numerically than some think and much stronger relatively in wealth, culture and effective leadership. Even if it . . . leans a little toward patrician reserve, [Boston] has inherited a high sense of responsibility and meets its obligations in the spirit of *noblesse oblige*.[11]

In the spirit of *noblesse oblige* social and educational reformers sought to transform the immigrants into good citizens. The city's eminent Unitarian ministers, Edward Everett Hale and James Freeman Clarke, led many of the reforms. Hemenway, a member of Clarke's congregation, along with others, embraced "faith and good works," the social gospel of Protestantism. They found faith in the progress of civilization inherent in the current interpretation of Christianity and Social Darwinism and committed themselves to good works in a variety of charitable and educational endeavors.[12] Hemenway's philanthropic career began during the Civil War when Hale appealed to her for funds to support a sewing project in a Boston public school. She gave generously to the cause and later contributed to the Soldiers' Memorial Society work in Wilmington.

After Hemenway employed Homans to assist her, they administered a wide variety of enterprises such as supporting a writer working under Henry James, enabling deserving young women to attend Vassar and Wellesley Colleges, contributing to Hampton Institute, aiding the Boston Teachers' Mutual Benefit Association, supporting archaeological expeditions to study American Indians, and maintaining the Hillside Home for poor white Protestant boys.[13] Hemenway entered personally into every major undertaking and analyzed each situation until she knew exactly what was required for its success. She did not expect returns without a proper investment and funded her projects amply. When Hale asked her to support sewing in the public schools, she not only provided supplies, but also furnished an instructor. To help preserve the American Indian culture, she made arrangements with Thomas A. Edison to procure a phonograph to record Indian languages.[14] In 1876, together with other women, including Mrs. Charles Francis Adams, Mrs. James Freeman Clarke, and Mrs. Alexander Agassiz, Hemenway helped buy back the Old South Meeting House which had been sold at auction. The women immediately instituted a lecture series which Homans managed. The lectures focused on the history of Boston and the United States, giving Bostonians, both school children and adults, the opportunity to learn about their city and nation.[15]

Gradually, Hemenway's interest focused on improving the lives of Boston's school children. She supported the new industrial education in which the students could learn skills to make them employable and to improve their daily lives. Hemenway believed that immigrant and working parents could not be relied upon to teach their children the proper care of the home and family for the United States of the future and that the public schools should assume this responsibility. After supporting the sewing project recommended by Hale, she turned her attention to the teaching of the proper selection and preparation of food. In the summer of 1885, under Hemenway's sponsorship, Homans conducted an experimental cooking program in the Starr King schoolhouse on Tennyson Street. Homans' program provided not only classes in food selection and preparation, but also free-hand drawing, embroidery, and carpentry. "It was a sight to remember, that basement room in the Starr King school, with a group of happy-faced girls busily wielding saw, plane and hammer, while the articles grew to perfectness under their willing hands."[16] Recognizing the importance of educating teachers in the basic sciences as well as the practical tasks of cooking, Hemenway established the Boston Normal School of Cookery, with Homans as the director. The school operated as a small, private institution with selective admission and a modest tuition.

Setting the highest possible standards for the school, Homans sought out the best available instruction, using Boston's educational institutions as a model rather than existing normal schools. The theoretical sciences which she considered so important were taught at the Massachusetts Institute of Technology by Ellen H. Richards, later known for her pioneering work in home economics, while the practical courses were conducted at the Rutland Street schoolhouse in rooms provided by the Boston School Board. Homans directed the Boston Normal School of Cookery for a year and a half. The school closed in 1890 because of the lack of demand for teachers, and when it reopened a year later, Louisa A. Nicholass was the new principal.

In the meantime, Hemenway and Homans turned their attention to another need of Boston's school children: health and vigor or "bodily education." Several incidents may have sparked Hemenway's interest in the topic. At one time she noticed the one-sided development of schoolboy cadets as they drilled with heavy muskets. In another instance she observed how easily a nurse lifted a heavy child and realized how few women in her social circle would be able to perform such a task. Finally, she "was led to consider what advantage would come to the human race, and especially to city populations if some well-considered system of bodily training could be made a part of our general education."[17] Reflecting the social and religious views of the period, Hemenway considered the body "a temple of God":

[Public education] deals chiefly with the intellectual and moral nature. Is it not possible to add to it subjects that will in no wise abate or abridge the results now accomplished, but rather will re-enforce them by reaching the intellect and the soul through that temple of God, the human body?

Is it not possible that public education should include such exercises as will give to the next and to subsequent generations better bodies, that shall be better fed and better clothed, and thus help to create better conditions for the indwelling of good character and the building up of better homes?[18]

Homans' explanation of Hemenway's interest in bodily education is similar. Speaking to BNSG and Wellesley alumnae in 1929, Homans recalled the reasons for promoting physical education:

From the outset we saw the need of something which would lift the life of the masses to a higher level of health and vigor, to a more sane and wholesome outlook, a more rational, self-controlled way of living. The comparatively new field of hygiene and physical education seemed more promising in these directions than anything else.[19]

With a deep belief that public education would improve the future of America, Hemenway and Homans resolved to introduce an exercise program in Boston's public schools as one means of bettering the students' lives. This decision led them to make a thorough and careful study of health and physical education in the 1880s.

They assembled scrapbooks of newspaper clippings, magazine articles, pamphlets, and other items on the subject. Interestingly, little in the scrapbooks records or notes the controversy which existed over women's education and vigorous exercise, both of which were considered questionable in the latter half of the nineteenth century. Many people firmly believed that women not only were biologically different from men, but also inferior beings, biologically, mentally, and socially, and unable to engage in higher education. Society, in general, considered women delicate and assigned them passive and submissive roles in the family and home.

It appears as if Homans and Hemenway, having decided to promote the health and vigor of girls as well as boys through exercise, included in their materials only articles which supported their position. However, to understand the impact Homans made on exercise and vigorous physical activity for women and women's professional education, it is necessary to examine the complex and intertwining arguments surrounding these issues.

According to the beliefs of the day, nature endowed each individual with a finite amount of a substance known as *force*. Every act, from threading a needle to studying Latin or chopping down a tree, required a portion of that force. While sleep permitted the restoration of force, it was possible to use up more force than that which was restored, thus initiating degeneration or debilitation of certain functions of the body. Three major bodily systems were recognized—the nutritive, the nervous, and the reproductive, all of which were supplied by and drew upon the body's force. While the nutritive and nervous systems functioned alike for men and women, the reproductive system obviously differed. Physiologists theorized that the development of a woman's reproductive system required more force than that required by a man. Frequently referred to as "women's peculiar organization," physicians and physiologists usually allotted four years in late adolescence to the growth and development of the female reproductive system. Clearly, force used to study school and college subjects lessened the force available to develop the reproductive system and, indeed, it was thought that too much study might interfere in the system's development.[20]

The physiology and medical knowledge of menstruation and childbearing remained a mystery in the nineteenth century and current medical practices led to difficult births, disease, and high death rates for both mothers and babies. Perhaps the most damaging account of the effects of higher education on young women came from E. H. Clarke in 1873. According to Clarke:

Girls, between the ages of fourteen and eighteen, must have sleep, not only for repair and growth, like boys, but for the additional task of constructing, or, more properly speaking, of developing and perfecting, then, a reproductive system,—the engine within an engine. The bearing of this physiological fact upon education is obvious. Work of the school is work of the brain. Work of the brain eats the brain away.[21]

He recounted case after case of educated young women who suffered ill health, mental breakdowns, and death as a result of mocking nature and following youthful whims. Miss E——, as Clarke calls one young woman, had a literary education. She appeared to have a sufficient supply of force to learn languages, natural sciences, philosophy, and mathematics while at the same time remaining in good physical condition. However, at 21 she began to suffer dysmenorrhea, and in a year or so developed acne and became despondent. She did not respond to treatment and, finally, was committed to an asylum. In another case, Clarke reports that Miss G—— died from overwork. "She was unable to make a good brain, that could stand the wear and tear of life, and a good reproductive system."[22] No wonder that M. Carey Thomas, president of Bryn Mawr College, confessed that "We were haunted in those early days by the clanging chains of that gloomy little specter, Dr. Edward H. Clarke's *Sex in Education.*"[23]

These beliefs only reinforced the idea that women were delicate creatures. Further, fashions of the day helped mold women into pale, inactive creatures who often had the "vapors" or "headaches." Three or four layers of undergarments which might include knee-length, bulky bloomers, a chemise, a corset made with bone or steel stays in an embroidered corset cover, long stockings, and one or two floor-length petticoats under the streetdress vastly restricted physical activity for women. Corsets, tightened until the waist measured no more than sixteen or eighteen inches, resulted in breathing difficulties and many health problems. One young woman is memorialized in a scrapbook assembled by Hemenway and Homans:

> Herein lies a girl
>   Whose brief, brief days
> Were briefer still
>   For wearing stays.[24]

Many women, especially of the working and lower middle classes, recognized the rhetoric of delicacy and fashion as an illusion. The realities of life in the decades following the Civil War, from the tragic loss of thousands of men in the war to the many changes in the industrial world, led more and more women to work outside the home. Manufacturing and new industries created many occupations in which women could be successful. By the 1880s women had entered a wide range of vocations including photography, auctioneering, stenography, telegraphing, dressmaking, clerking, wood engraving, tinning, and poultry farming.[25] These women and others who had to care for their own homes, clean, wash, make clothes, cook, and look after their husbands and children could not afford the luxuries of delicacy and high fashion. Though dismissed by these women, the cult of delicacy lingered as an ideal and became a major issue as middle and upperclass girls sought an education comparable to that of men.

Allegations such as those made by Clarke raised questions about the health of the students in the newly established colleges for women. When Mary Lyon opened Mount Holyoke Seminary in South Hadley, Massachusetts, in 1837, she required the students to perform domestic duties to avoid being dependent on hired help and to promote student health through worthwhile activity. The domestic work was supplemented by daily mile-long walks and twenty minutes of calisthenics. Matthew Vassar's prospectus for Vassar College in 1861 began with the need for good health as a basis for developing mental and moral power. He appointed Dr. Alida C. Avery professor of physiology and hygiene and another woman to instruct physical training. In 1875 Henry Fowle Durant, founder of Wellesley College, followed Vassar's model and procured a woman physician to teach hygiene and physiology and an instructor to supervise required exercises. The intent of both Vassar and Durant was to ensure healthy, vigorous women able to attend classes regularly and undertake collegiate work comparable to that of men.[26]

While the proponents of exercise for girls and women proclaimed its benefits, recreational physical activities in the form of sport raised other questions. More and more girls and women enjoyed archery, croquet, rowing, bicycling, and other outdoor recreational pursuits. Although some critics acknowledged that the new sportswomen had increased vigor, others noted that they now neglected their social and familial responsibilities. Young women who played tennis, rowed around a lake, or bicycled in the country had less time to nurse and visit the sick, make peace among family members, tutor young brothers, and help make the family clothes. "When Clara tired with a walk beyond two miles, Clara took flowers and books to her sick or less fortunate friends. Now that she can 'manage twenty miles easily,' [on her bicycle] her sick and less fortunate friends miss her."[27] Critics reinforced the views that less vigorous women who stayed at home and cared for others were more desirable than active sportswomen and were, perhaps, even more feminine.

In spite of women working outside the home and the gradual opening of higher education to women, views of women changed very little. Hemenway and Homans joined the reformers who believed that exercise improved women's health. Sport for women was not an immediate issue, but one which Homans would face in the future. They discovered that a number of different physical training or physical education programs existed in the United States, and their next problem was to determine which exercise program or system would be most suitable for Boston's public schools.

3

Victorian Views of Exercise

In Boston in the mid-1880s, several different exercise programs or systems were practiced in local colleges and gymnasiums. Dudley Allen Sargent devised his own system for Harvard University; the Young Men's Christian Association (YMCA) provided an exercise program under the supervision of Robert J. Roberts; the local Turnverein offered German gymnastics; and Mary Allen operated a private gymnasium and training school, using still another program of exercise. Hemenway and Homans decided that none of these programs met their criteria and, instead, chose the little-known Swedish system. Their decision can be better understood by examining briefly the current views of exercise in this country and the programs found in Boston.[1]

Although there had been a brief flurry of interest in exercise and fitness in the early decades of the century, sustained interest in physical vigor and improved health through systematic exercise did not occur until the 1870s and 1880s. The early interest in fitness and exercise is attributed in part to three young German refugees, students of Friedrich Ludwig Jahn (1778–1852), who had been active in the Turner movement in Germany. Jahn, considered the father of German gymnastics, created an exercise system based on vigorous exercises and feats performed on specially designed apparatus. Underlying his movement were strong political overtones, stressing German cultural unity and the defense of the fatherland. Choosing the German root *Turn* rather than a Greek or Latin root, Jahn created a special vocabulary to emphasize the national character of his movement. He designated members of the movement as *Turners*. They gathered in a *Turnplatz* for outdoor exercises or in a *Turnverein* for indoor exercises. As Jahn's movement became more political, it was outlawed in Germany and many members fled the country. Three young reformers, Charles Beck, Charles Follen, and Francis Lieber reached the United States in the 1820s, at a time when a few educators and medical doctors had become interested in bodily exercise.

In 1825 Beck joined the faculty of the experimental Round Hill School for boys in Northampton, Massachusetts, where he taught gymnastics and other sports as part of the school's innovative curriculum. Follen was appointed instructor in German at Harvard University and, in response to student interest, introduced Jahn's German gymnastics at Harvard. Prominent Bostonians such as Dr. John Warren, Professor George Ticknor, John S. Foster, John A. Lowell, Daniel Webster, and Josiah Quincy believed in the new exercises and sponsored an outdoor gymnasium which Follen directed. He resigned a year later and was replaced by Lieber who, in addition to organizing the gymnastics programs, started a swimming school. Beck left Round Hill School in 1830 and two years later joined the Harvard faculty. Interest in Lieber's gymnasium and swimming school faded and he, too, turned to teaching other subjects. The careers of these young Germans should be viewed not as a means to promote the vigor and health of United States men and boys, but rather as a way to establish themselves in a new country.

As thousands of other German immigrants arrived in the mid-nineteenth century, Turner societies sprang up across the country, maintaining German ethnic traditions, and also focusing on the importance of the new immigrants becoming good American citizens. These programs were usually housed in a local Turnverein that included not only a gymnasium and classrooms, but also a restaurant. (These buildings acted as gathering places for German-Americans.) In addition to the gymnastic program, Turner societies frequently offered classes in drama, music, and art. German gymnastics, as the Turner system came to be called in this country, stressed formal exercises or calisthenics, performing on heavy apparatus such as the vaulting horse, and using light apparatus like sticks or wands, dumbbells, and clubs. The system also included athletic activities such as running, jumping, and throwing. German gymnastics, aiming at general physical culture, classified its exercises according to strength, ability, and age, and, in daily workouts, proceeded from simple to more difficult movements.

In order to obtain teachers for the Turnvereins in America, the Turners organized a normal school in the 1860s. The school lasted a few weeks and was conducted first in one city and then another, finally settling in Milwaukee, Wisconsin. The curriculum consisted of German gymnastics, German and English languages, history, basic sciences, and the principles of the Turner organization. Outside of German ethnic communities, the interest in exercise sparked by Beck, Follen, Lieber and some interested Americans generally declined within a few years. However, the importance of exercise for health and vigor continued to be discussed in the current literature and came to the attention of mid-century reformers.

Physicians, educators, and social reformers observed that men and boys, living in the cities and employed in sedentary jobs, no longer displayed the strong muscular bodies resulting from the chores required for daily living on a farm or in a small village, but which were unnecessary in the city. Although some reformers suggested outdoor pursuits and sports to counteract the debilitating effects of city living, many physicians and educators recommended periods of formal exercise which would systematically develop each part of the body. Some even suggested that girls and women might benefit from moderate exercise. For example, Warren urged that young women engage in walking, dancing, exercising with light apparatus, and playing battledore with the left hand as well as the right hand.[2] Although his view was not widely held at that time, it was shared by a growing number of educators and reformers who wished to improve the citizenry of the young nation. As noted in the previous chapter, Lyon insisted on daily exercise when Mount Holyoke Seminary opened in 1837. Catharine Beecher, the educator and reformer, also included exercise programs in her schools, but she was more influential through her writings. With the exception of Mount Holyoke and a few other academies, women's exercise programs of this early period, like the men's programs, faded for a few decades.

By the 1850s and 1860s attention again turned to the deteriorating vigor of the citizenry. Beecher stressed the need for good hygienic practices, knowledge of the human body, and regular exercise to benefit each person.[3] During the 1860s "strength seekers" commanded considerable support among men. They promoted lifting weights and using other apparatus designed to increase strength. The most popular strength seeker, George Barker Windship, greatly influenced Robert Jefferies Roberts' exercise programs in Boston's YMCA.

Dioclesian Lewis (1823–1886), a popular and flamboyant Boston lecturer on temperance, health, and exercise, strongly opposed the health-through-strength movement. He devised new gymnastics suitable for everyone—men, boys, girls, and women—using light equipment such as wands, Indian Clubs, wooden rings, and two-pound dumbbells. His system became popular and, in 1861, he opened the Boston Normal Institute for Physical Education to train teachers in his method. The school closed seven years later, having graduated 421 students, about an equal number of men and women. Through his school Dio Lewis' new gymnastics spread over New England and reached many parts of the country.[4]

The popular journalist Thomas Wentworth Higginson agreed that the mechanization of modern life lessened the need for daily physical activity and increased the need to seek other means of maintaining vigor. He reminded his readers that "all the coarser tasks are constantly being handed over to the German or Irish immigrant,—not because the American cannot do the particular thing required, but because he is promoted to something more intellectual." He also assigned a moral quality to exercises which "give to energy and daring a legitimate channel, supply the place of war, gambling, licentiousness, highway robbery, and office seeking."[5] He encouraged men and boys to engage in exercise to replace the physical activity formerly necessary in their daily chores, to be morally pure, and to acquire the physical vigor essential for American manhood.

These ideals also characterized the first college physical education program, instituted at Amherst College in western Massachusetts. In 1861 Amherst College appointed Dr. Edward Hitchcock (1828–1911) to teach Amherst students the proper care of the body as well as exercises to increase, and then maintain, bodily vigor for optimal mental and physical development. Hitchcock's plan for each exercise period consisted of fifteen or twenty minutes of exercise in which the students might use dumbbells or heavier weights depending on their capabilities. After these exercises, the students executed formal marching, and then finished with ten minutes of exercises such as running, tumbling, or lifting weights. The Amherst plan soon became the model for other programs. As institutions acknowledged their responsibility for their students' health and vigor, they turned to medical doctors to introduce and supervise exercise programs. By the 1880s, when Homans made her exhaustive study of physical education, Hitchcock was considered one of the leading authorities in the field.

While the Amherst program purported to ensure the vigor for each student's optimal mental and physical development, the first exercise programs in the early women's colleges served another purpose. As noted in the previous chapter, the proponents of women's higher education used exercise programs to condition women so that they could endure a daily schedule of regular classes and rigorous academic assignments. They followed Amherst's lead and appointed physicians, women physicians to be sure, to supervise the students' health and to teach basic hygienic practices. However, an instructor other than the physician usually conducted the exercise programs. When Vassar College in Poughkeepsie, New York, opened in 1865, one of the buildings, the "Calisthenium," housed a gymnasium, a bowling alley, and riding facilities. Ten years later, when Wellesley College opened, College Hall included a small gymnasium. Henry Fowle Durant, the college's founder, also built a tennis court, provided boats for rowing on the college lake, and constructed paths for walking through the large campus. The provision for recreational sports on these campuses reflected the growing interest of women in sport.

Amherst, Vassar, and Wellesley, all undergraduate liberal arts colleges, did not concern themselves with the preparation of gymnastics teachers. In 1879, when Harvard sought a director for its new Hemenway Gymnasium, a gift of Mary Hemenway's son, it followed Amherst and appointed a physician, Dr. Dudley Allen Sargent (1849–1924). Some twenty years younger than Hitchcock, Sargent held the M.D. degree from Yale and had managed a private gymnasium in New York City before coming to Harvard. Sargent not only directed physical training for the undergraduate men, but also instituted an exercise program for the women of the "Harvard Annex," a teacher training course for women, and a summer school for men and women teachers. In addition, he conducted research, was active in professional organizations, and served on a number of university committees.

According to Sargent, an exercise program should produce a symmetrical and well-developed body. He invented "pulley-weight" or "developing" machines which exercised specific parts of the body such as the back, arm, hand, or thigh muscles. Based on the results of an individual examination, he prescribed exercises on his machines for each student. Sargent's system and machines soon became popular and widely used.

Within a year after the Hemenway Gymnasium opened, the women of the Harvard Annex or the Society for the Collegiate Instruction of Women, later called Radcliffe College, persuaded Sargent to teach them gymnastics. He soon realized that he would need assistance and offered to accept a few women to train as teachers. In 1881 Sargent remodeled an old carriage house for the women's program and named it the Sanatory Gymnasium. Although Sargent did not exclude men from his Normal School, very few enrolled. In response to the increasing demand for both men and women physical educators, he began the Harvard Summer School of Physical Education in 1887. The student body—army and navy officers, lawyers, physicians, college professors, and school superintendents—reflected the growing interest in physical training.

By this time more and more educational, philanthropic, and private institutions offered exercise programs, increasing the need for teachers. In addition to Dr. Sargent's Normal School, two other teacher-training schools were established in the mid-1880s, one in Brooklyn, New York, and one in Springfield,

Massachusetts. In 1885, following the pattern of Amherst and Harvard, Adelphi Academy appointed Dr. William G. Anderson (1860–1947) director of physical training. The following year Anderson established the Brooklyn Normal School for Physical Training, which was open to both men and women and offered instruction in basic sciences and German, Swedish, and American gymnastics.

During the years following the Civil War it had become evident that many young men visited the YMCA to exercise in the gymnasium rather than to receive the message of Christianity. By 1887, the demand for gymnasium directors had became so great that the Training School for Christian Workers, later Springfield College, in Springfield, Massachusetts, organized a physical department, appointing Roberts, from the Boston YMCA, and Luther Halsey Gulick (1865–1918) to teach in the department. Within a year Roberts returned to Boston, leaving young Gulick in charge. Gulick, who became a widely recognized leader in physical education, instituted an imaginative curriculum which included sport as well as gymnastics.

Another gymnastic teacher training program, the Allen School, opened in Boston in 1878. Mary Allen (1841–1925) left the Boston public schools to operate a private gymnasium employing her own system that promoted athletic exercises and the harmonious development of the body. She offered a four-year graded course that, according to its description, could be adapted to individuals ranging from six-year-old children to elderly women. Her equipment included Indian clubs, bars, flying rings, and other light and heavy apparatus. Newspaper articles attest to the popularity of her gymnasium. Her students praised her work enthusiastically. In addition to the exercise and sport programs, the Allen Gymnasium purported to offer a two-year normal course of instruction including anatomy, physiology, and the science of movement.

Although the exercise programs in vogue in the 1880s all focused on improving and maintaining health and vigor, they varied considerably. In Boston, the Turnverein utilized German gymnastics; at Harvard, Sargent employed his own developing machines for individually prescribed exercises; Roberts' program at the YMCA reflected the influence of the strength-seekers, especially Windship; and Allen offered her general exercise program. Homans and Hemenway found none of these programs satisfactory.

The strong cultural overtones of the German system would be inconsistent with Hemenway's educational philosophy. Sargent's development machines exercised only underdeveloped parts of the body and did not provide an overall program, much less one suitable for children. The machines themselves were costly, required special installation and maintenance, and would not be suited to the average public school classrooms. Based on improving strength, the YMCA program appealed to young men and would not be appropriate for young girls and boys. While no specific letter or comment exists explaining why Allen's work was not chosen, it is possible that the commercialism of her gymnasium was distasteful to Hemenway. Whether or not any personal animosity existed between Hemenway and Allen is not known, but it was the Allen program that became an obstacle to Homans' and Hemenway's plans to incorporate Swedish gymnastics in Boston's public schools.

The Ling, or Swedish, system that Homans and Hemenway selected was not new to Boston. It had been proposed twenty years earlier by Superintendent John D. Philbrick. In 1861 a report recommended that the Ling system be introduced "into all our schools, and . . . made an obligatory branch of education." As a result, Professor Lewis B. Munroe conducted classes in both physical training and voice culture.[6] In the intervening years, interest in the program declined and, by the 1880s, the Swedish system of gymnastics was apparently unknown in Boston.

About this time, a young, likable advocate of Swedish gymnastics, Baron Nils Posse (1862–1895) arrived in Boston with the hopes of interesting Bostonians in his country's gymnastic program. Born in Sweden and graduated from the Royal Central Institute of Gymnastics in 1885, he left for the United States shortly thereafter. While one story suggests than an acquaintance of Hemenway told her about Posse's work and arranged an introduction, Posse himself explains that "In 1887 [I] published a little pamphlet entitled 'Medical Gymnastics,' which chanced to fall into the hands of a noted philanthropist [Hemenway]."[7] Hemenway and Homans found the exercises in the Swedish system completely satisfactory for their purpose.

Invented in Sweden by Per Henrik Ling in the early part of the century, but constantly improved over the years, the Swedish system of gymnastics classified body movements into basic groups and followed an unchanging order in daily workouts. The "day's order," a carefully planned progression based on biological and psychological theories of the period, was educationally sound. First came warm-up exercises, followed by backward flexions, hanging from a bar, balance and shoulder exercises, and abdominal, lateral-trunk, leg, and respiratory exercises. Within the day's order a wide variety of exercises from simple to complex and from easy to difficult had been devised, so that each lesson held the students' attention. Further, the exercises could be modified for classrooms and learned and conducted by the classroom teacher.

The Swedish system met all of Hemenway and Homans' criteria. It had been well tested for over half a century and had been adopted in other countries such as England. The exercises had an infinite variety, had been graded from simple to complex, and could be used from the primary grades through high school. The Swedish exercises encouraged good posture and were designed to foster health in children and young people and not to train soldiers or produce athletes.

Based on their careful study of exercise in the 1880s, Homans and Hemenway selected the Swedish system of gymnastics as the exercise program best suited to the Boston public schools. They still faced the tasks of persuading the school authorities to adopt the Swedish system of gymnastics and of providing teachers for the new program.

4

The Struggle for Swedish Gymnastics in the Boston Schools

During 1888 and 1889 Homans and Hemenway launched a two-pronged attack to convince the Boston School Committee to adopt Swedish gymnastics in the Boston public schools. In the fall of 1888, Hemenway, at her own expense, hired Posse to train public school teachers in the Swedish system. In April, 1889, she offered to train another group of teachers so that Swedish gymnastics could be tested in more schools. Also, to call attention to "bodily" or physical education as a national need rather than a local one, Hemenway convened a national conference in the interest of physical training in Boston in November, 1889. The conference, now generally referred to as "the 1889 Conference," proved to be a landmark in the history of physical education.

The fact that two women, one a philanthropist and one an able administrator, planned and carried out such a conference in the 1880s makes it even more remarkable. Hemenway and Homans succeeded in procuring a hall at the Massachusetts Institute of Technology (MIT) for the meetings held on November 29 and 30, 1889, and in gathering the major authorities on physical education to present their views on the subject. United States Commissioner of Education, William T. Harris, presided and Edward M. Hartwell (1850–1922) made the opening address. The American Association for the Advancement of Physical Education (AAAPE) rescheduled its 1889 meeting to permit members to attend the conference; attendance was further bolstered by holding the conference at the same time as the Massachusetts Teachers Association meeting in Boston.

Local support of the conference was impressive. President Francis A. Walker of MIT, President William F. Warren of Boston University, and President Helen Shafer of Wellesley College supported the event. Other sponsors included Alice Freeman Palmer, Kate Gannett Wells, and John W. Dickinson of the Massachusetts State Board of Education; Edwin P. Seaver, the Superintendent of the Boston Public Schools; eighteen members of the Boston School Committee; a number of well-known Boston physicians; and many socially prominent Boston women. The impressive array of educators, physicians, philanthropists, and socialites lent an air of authority to the conference.

Homans enthusiastically described the conference in an informal letter to General Armstrong of Hampton Institute in Virginia:

The German[,] Swedish and different American Systems will be presented by means of papers and classwork—Drs. Hartwell of Johns Hopkins, Sargent of Cambridge, Wey of Elmira, Hitchcock of Amherst, Prof. Mentzner (German) of N.Y., Nils Posse (Swedish—our instructor) all will present papers. Com. Wm. T. Harris will preside and leading educators & Drs. from everywhere will be here—Will you come?[1]

Although the announced purpose of the conference was to discuss the existing systems of gymnastics in relation to the needs of schools, it is likely that Hemenway and Homans believed that the Swedish system would stand out as the best exercise system for the Boston public schools. Obviously, they organized the program to present the Swedish system in a favorable light. Following Hartwell's opening address first German gymnastics and then Swedish gymnastics were presented. Carl Eberhard of the Boston Athletic Club Gymnasium read a paper on the German system prepared by Heinrich Metzner of the New York Turnverein, who was unable to attend. Claes J. Enebuske and Posse both addressed the advantages of the Swedish system. Then Hitchcock, the outstanding authority from Amherst, and Sargent from Harvard described their programs of college physical education.

After presentations on the major programs of the period, and almost as if to provide contrasts to Swedish gymnastics, representatives of less well-known programs completed the agenda. C. W. Emerson, president of the Monroe College of Oratory, outlined his principles of physical culture. Dr. Hamilton D. Wey spoke on the benefits of physical training for "defective" children and youthful criminals. Finally, Hobart Moore expounded the advantages of military drill as a means of physical training. In light of the status of physical education in the 1880s, the program is an admirable overview of the field at that time. While the younger men, Gulick and Anderson, did not present papers, they were among the conferees who spoke freely during the discussions.

About 2,000 people attended the conference. A local newsman's description of the audience alludes to teachers who had come to Boston for the Massachusetts Teachers Association meeting but also shows the interest of women in physical education: "Fifteen persons out of every twenty present were New England school marms. About one-fifth wore spectacles, mostly hooked behind the ears; one-tenth were young, pretty as pictures and as smart as lightning, and one-twentieth produced visual agony."[2] While the majority of the audience were from New England, conferees came from New York City, Brooklyn, Washington, D.C., and from many outstanding men's and women's colleges. Even Baron Pierre de Coubertin, founder of the modern Olympic Games, who was visiting in the United States at that time, attended as the representative of the French Educational Reform Association. Reporters from Boston's papers, national journals, and newspapers as far away as Baltimore published accounts of the conference.

In his opening remarks Harris warned the conferees "to avoid all narrow interpretations of our subject" and raised a number of questions concerning the "new" physical education, which, according to Harris, began with Hitchcock at Amherst in the 1860s.[3] Hartwell's keynote address presented the thesis that "bodily exercise constitutes so considerable and necessary an element in all human training that physical training is entitled to be recognized and provided for as an integral and indispensable factor in the education of all children and youth."[4] He distinguished between gymnastics and athletic sports, noting that they are "inadequate for the purposes of a thorough-going and broad system of bodily education."[5] Being careful not to favor either system publicly, Hartwell suggested that "a careful study of the German and Swedish systems of school gymnastics will be found an indispensable preliminary step for those who propose to organize a natural, rational, safe and effective system of American physical education."[6]

As expected, the speakers for German gymnastics and Swedish gymnastics extolled the merits of each system. According to Metzner, the German system stressed the all-around development of the individual, was adaptable to classwork, and offered carefully organized lessons to procure the desired result. The audience was reminded that neither the paper nor the short exhibition which followed could adequately demonstrate the values of the system.

Next came the papers on Swedish gymnastics. First Enebuske and then Posse lectured on the unique aspects of the Ling system. Enebuske proposed the term "physical educator" for the specialist in physical training. He listed three requirements of physical training: first, developing the whole body harmoniously; second, promoting strength, dexterity, and efficiency; and third, improving bodily health. He explained how Ling's pedagogical gymnastics met these criteria and emphasized the need for physical training in the educational system. Posse analyzed the physiological bases and the methods employed in teaching Swedish gymnastics, calling the system rational and practical and noting that it had survived for almost a century because of its merits. He emphasized that the day's order, a strict progression of exercises from the simplest to the most complex, made the system adaptable to educational institutions. Following his paper, a class of ladies demonstrated Swedish gymnastics.

The conference then turned to Hitchcock and Sargent, who represented programs designed by American educators. Hitchcock pointed out that physical education at Amherst College enabled the students to maintain or improve vital bodily functions for the greatest efficiency of their intellectual and spiritual lives. After a thorough anthropometric examination of each student and lectures on general health, the men took part in exercise classes four times a week. In addition, both light and heavy apparatus were available for individual students who wished to develop various parts of the body. Outdoor sports were encouraged but were not considered a substitute for gymnastic exercises.

Sargent explained that his system originated from observing the muscular development resulting from certain labors such as blacksmithing and wood-chopping. In his search for a symmetrical body, he devised exercises that developed specific parts of the body. He based his Harvard program on meticulous examinations of each student, including photographs. After the examination, Sargent devised an individual prescription of exercises and apparatus work for each man. He explained that the student competed only with himself and improved at his own rate. After six months the student was examined again and received new suggestions. Sargent remarked that athletics at Harvard were managed by the students themselves, but that each student procured a certificate from the director of the gymnasium before he participated in a sport. He also described his summer school for teachers and his private gymnasium where he taught a normal class for women teachers. He closed his remarks stating:

What America most needs is the happy combination . . . [of] the strength-giving qualities of the German gymnasium, the active and energetic properties of the English sports, the grace and suppleness acquired from the French calisthenics, and the beautiful poise and mechanical precision of the Swedish free movements, all regulated, systematized, and adapted to our peculiar needs and institutions.[7]

Following each address and exhibition the conferees expressed their opinions and debated the issues. It became clear that most conferees believed in the merits of exercise, but not in any one system. Foreseeing the future, Dr. Helen Putnam of Vassar College proposed that each child have a medical examination before engaging in any exercise program. Dr. Alice T. Hall of the Women's College of Baltimore, now Goucher College, spoke out in favor of the Swedish movements because of the results they produced. Seaver favored out-of-doors work, commenting that the Swedish system required too much mental attention and suggesting some American modifications of the Swedish system. Anderson stated that neither the German nor the Swedish system suited the American people. Most of those present appeared to favor an American version of existing exercise programs.

Perhaps the most pragmatically American reaction came from Wellesley's Lucille Eaton Hill, who startled the conference with her outburst, "I hate the word system,—don't you?" She described her system as "eclectic"—taking the best ideas from each. She also urged special consideration for girls to be sure that they received adequate training.[8] Dr. Carolyn C. Ladd of Bryn Mawr College stressed the need for physical training of girls regardless of the system—"Swedish, American, or whatever it might be."[9] The Boston physician Dr. Walter Channing suggested that no specific system be adopted, but that excellent well-trained teachers be appointed. "We have got to take the best things out of each system and mix them all up and apply them as we see the need."[10] When asked to give his opinion, de Coubertin extolled the virtues of the English athletic sport system.

At the beginning of the second day, Seaver proposed the following resolution:

Resolved, That a Committee of eleven be appointed to take into consideration the best means of presenting in the common schools the method or methods of physical education; this Committee to be appointed either by the chair or by the audience as shall be thought best.[11]

The chair of the conference, Harris, appointed the following committee: Edwin P. Seaver, Superintendent of Schools, Boston; J. W. Dickinson, Secretary, Board of Education, Boston; Edward M. Hartwell, M.D., Baltimore; D. A. Sargent, M.D., Harvard College, Cambridge; Miss Amy Morris Homans, Boston; Ray Greene Huling, New Bedford; James A. Page, Boston; C. G. Meleney, Superintendent of Schools, Somerville; Prof. Lucille E. Hill, Wellesley College; Prof. J. B. Powell, Washington, D.C.; and Mrs. Louisa P. Hopkins, Boston. At the close of the conference, another resolution was offered:

Resolved, That the most cordial thanks of this Conference be extended to Mrs. Hemenway and to Miss Homans for the generosity and large-mindedness that led them to undertake and guide this Conference; and to express our conviction that not only the Boston public schools, but the whole cause of physical education in America, has received a great impetus from this meeting, which is the result of their labors.[12]

The motion passed unanimously and the conference adjourned. In a final gesture of social graciousness, the conferees were entertained at a reception at the Hotel Brunswick. A local newspaper described the event: "The attendance was large, and three hours were pleasantly spent in a social manner. An elegant collation was served, and there was music. The affair was entirely informal, but none the less pleasant."[13]

The committee of eleven, appointed by Harris at the vote of the conference, was never heard from. In actuality, there was no one or nobody to receive and act on a report. It is not known whether or not the committee met, but no report or reference to the committee has been found except that in the conference proceedings.[14]

The Conference in the Interest of Physical Training thrust Homans into a position of authority in the emerging field of physical education. The conference brought together the most prestigious scholars and administrators in physical education, arranged an open forum to debate the merits of the various gymnastic systems, and called attention to the need for physical as well as mental education. Homans was now acquainted with the leaders in the field—Hitchcock, Sargent, Hartwell, Anderson, Gulick, and others. In addition, she had met the prominent women in physical education—Ladd from Bryn Mawr, Hall from the Women's College of Baltimore, and Hill from Wellesley, all of whom had expressed their opinions about gymnastics and physical training for women. It is interesting to speculate whether or not their remarks influenced the manner in which Homans molded BNSG and physical education for women.

Local and regional newspapers reported the conference, calling attention to the academic nature and scientific bases of physical education. National journals carried articles discussing the importance of the papers read at the conference. At a time when the literature on physical education consisted of one or two modest journals, a few pamphlets and some articles, Hemenway published a detailed report of the conference and distributed it widely, thus adding to the meager literature in the field.

In the meantime, Hemenway's and Homans' efforts to have the Boston School Committee adopt Swedish gymnastics burst into a full-scale public controversy. The debate centered on Hemenway's offer to train public school teachers in Swedish gymnastics at her own expense. Posse's success with the first class of teachers led Hemenway to propose to train "free of expense to the city of Boston, one hundred public-school teachers, who may be permitted to use the system in their school work, thus enabling . . . educators in general, to decide upon its [the Ling system of gymnastics] merits by actual results produced upon the school children within the environment of the schoolroom."[15] Hemenway's offer was referred to the committee on hygiene which reported back to the School Board on September 25, recommending "That the Ling system of gymnastics be the authorized system of physical training in the public schools, and that it be introduced into them as soon as the teachers are prepared to conduct the exercises."[16] Just when it appeared that Hemenway and Homans had achieved their goal, Dr. Caroline E. Hastings, a member of the committee, charged Hemenway with going too far in promoting Swedish gymnastics:

May I ask that it [Hemenway's offer] be laid on the table, until the subject of the Ling system is taken up? . . . I think we had better wait until we know we are going to adopt the Ling system, and then we can provide for it. But I think we should pause before we put this system in . . . and in speaking as I do, I intend no disrespect for Mrs. Hemenway or Miss Homans, who is her exponent. We have taken a class of a hundred here and a hundred there, and now it is proposed to go farther in the matter. I think it is time for us to pause, and now I ask the board to pause.[17]

Hastings supposedly opposed the plan, not because she objected to physical training or the Ling system, but because she believed the matter had not been thoroughly investigated and no plan for implementing the system had been proposed. In the ensuing deliberations, however, it became clear that Hastings believed that Allen's system had not been sufficiently considered. The debate flared into a public controversy between the Swedish and Allen systems. The committee hearings, fully reported in the daily newspapers, attracted the attention of readers who joined in the fray. One reader, signing as Constant Reader, expostulated:

Why was this [Ling] system actually put into the schools without authority from either the committee in charge or the School Board at large? Evidently for no other reason than that a well-meaning, benevolent, but in this case misguided, lady brought her powerful influence to bear on the introduction of it alone, to the exclusion of anything better there might be. . . . It seems as if the ridiculous position in which the school committee in question has been placed already, . . . is not to end here. They are to indorse and are made to dance attendance on a conference called, not by the School Board, but by the very lady referred to or her representative, in order to be instructed there. . . . Do the eminent gentlemen who have kindly consented to appear and to speak at this conference realize who called them, and what they are called for?[18]

The discussions and arguments continued on both sides. At one meeting of the School Board, Winship reported that in over 50 grammar schools, 23 masters had no special choice. The Ling system was favored by 22 masters and the Monroe system by five. Hastings argued against the Ling system, labeling it "very old," and for Allen's system which she believed to be more modern and adaptable to the present-day schools. The committee arranged demonstrations of the various systems and then cancelled some of them. Reports suggest that unannounced meetings were conducted and unpleasant accusations made. Allen received some criticism when she refused to consider partial adoption of her system and insisted on instructing all the teachers if her system were selected by the School Board.[19] Reflecting a growing impatience with the controversy, the School Committee voted to assign the subject of gymnastics to the next School Board.

When the next board convened, a new Committee on Physical Training was formed which included Hastings; however, she sent word to the board that she would be unable to attend the meetings. Without her, the newly formed committee reported favorably for the Ling, or Swedish, system and, in June, 1890, the School Board voted to introduce Swedish gymnastics into the public schools.[20] The committee also authorized a new position of director of physical training and appointed Hartwell to the post.

During those years of discussions, Homans studied bodily education and became an authority on the subject. Neither a physician nor an instructor of gymnastics, she had read everything available, corresponded with the authorities, listened to them, and, perhaps, conversed with them at the 1889 conference, and now she joined them professionally. The conference, with its lively discussions, sharpened her awareness of the need for a rigorous scientific academic background as well as practical work in gymnastics. Women evinced a great interest in the conference and Homans may have begun to envision the role of physical education in improving women's health and, thus, future generations. Homans foresaw not the need for normal school training available at Sargent's normal school and Allen's gymnasium, not the German program with its ethnic overtones, and not Anderson's broad program of activities, but a growing need for a school to educate women to conduct gymnasiums in colleges and universities. These women leaders would, in turn, teach other women to strive for better physical health and vigor, part of the good life which should be the right of all women.

5

The Founding of the Boston Normal School of Gymnastics

The Boston Normal School of Gymnastics (BNSG) opened officially in the fall of 1889 on Park Street in Boston. We do not know how many students registered for the new school, but two years later, in 1891, twelve women were graduated. These twelve became the first of hundreds who were educated under Homans' carefully thought out approach to the professional education of women. During the past few years Homans had made a thorough study of physical training and gymnastic systems or exercises and, through the 1889 conference, had come to know the authorities in physical education—Hartwell, Hitchcock, Sargent, Posse for the Swedish system, and Metzner for the German system. It may have been fortuitous that Homans, with her background in education and administration, entered this relatively new field at the time that it was on the edge of expansion and acceptance. She brought to it a perspective that permitted her to discern the values of physical education as well as the difficulties it faced.

As is true of so much of Homans' work, there is no evidence from the mid-1880s which sets forth her views on physical education. However, retrospective remarks, made in 1929 when she was 80 years old, reveal "the policy, the ideals and principles upon which the school was founded and its work was carried on." The object was to raise "the level of health and vigor" of the masses so they could enjoy a more wholesome life. Homans noted that:

The teacher has unsurpassed opportunities to present the ideals of "the good life" as regards health and efficiency, thoroughness, perseverance and high quality of action, unselfish, courteous and honorable conduct. These are illustrated and exemplified not only in the activities, but through the teacher's example and influence and they can and should be made to carry over and be applied in daily living.

Homans reminded her audience that "in the activities of physical education the young human reveals and expresses his fundamental self perhaps more truly and more completely than in any other way."[1] Even in the 1880s she stressed the importance of developing the physical and moral capacities of the individual; for her, physical education made important contributions to such development, leading to a more wholesome life. Thus, Homans interpreted physical education as a means of increasing the health, vigor, and moral uprightness of the masses.

These lofty ideas remained the center of Homans' life, but her well-ordered mind and businesslike approach to her endeavors led her to seek practical means for achieving her goals. She moved quickly beyond Hemenway's original object of preparing gymnastics teachers for Boston's public schools to creating a national effort to better women's lives through physical education. She intended to make BNSG the leading normal school of gymnastics, training generations of teachers who, in turn, would train their students to spread physical education as part of the good life.

Homans believed the difficulties which physical education faced centered on the poor academic background of teachers and the lack of a plan to disseminate physical education throughout the country. Sargent, Anderson, and, perhaps, Allen, offered academic subjects in their schools' curricula, but these institutions graduated relatively few students. Although Sargent and Anderson held medical degrees, most gymnastics teachers and gymnasium directors had little or no formal education. Many Bostonians could still remember Abram Molineaux Hewlett, Harvard's first gymnasium director, who had been a boxing teacher in Worcester, Massachusetts, and was described as "a mulatto, of very fine physique, and of reputable and estimable character. He was . . . a fair gymnast and a remarkably good teacher of boxing."[2]

From her study of existing physical education programs, Homans knew that a strong science background similar to that required for the study of medicine was essential, but that it should focus on understanding the body and searching for ways to improve health rather than on treating disease. She also realized the necessity of selecting students who would be models for the healthy, vigorous life they would expound. At some point, and certainly by 1890, Homans made plans for women to be central to the success of her mission. Women had evinced a great interest in the Conference in the Interest of Physical Training and had long found careers in teaching. Homans anticipated the additional difficulties they would confront in the field of physical education.

First, the capacity of women to undertake advanced study in sciences and daily strenuous exercise remained in doubt. Second, and perhaps more important to the success of Homans' plans, the ability of women to hold positions on college faculties was largely untested and questionable. Homans solved the first issue not by offering her students easy courses and mild physical activity, but by instituting a probationary period in which she could exclude applicants who might be unsuccessful in any course, whether in the gymnasium or classroom. She firmly believed that strenuous physical activity benefited healthy women when undertaken as part of a planned regimen of study, exercise, and rest. Homans approached the second problem with an equally firm policy, but only after carefully examining a new phenomenon in the late-nineteenth century: women in the professional world.

Homans knew that BNSG graduates would be among the vanguard of early professional women who did not follow the expected path of marrying or remaining at home to care for aging parents. Many women who worked outside the home held minor, low-paying positions as stenographers, clerks, nurses, or elementary school teachers. Even several years after BNSG had been in existence, very few women held teaching positions in colleges and universities.

1897–1898	Teachers Employed in the United States	
	Men	Women
Common Schools	131,750	277,443
High Schools	8,542	9,399
Colleges & Universities	11,571	1,577[3]

Homans expected her students to be administrators, not assistants or instructors. She clearly understood that they might be either the only woman or one of very few women to hold a position of authority on a college campus. In such a situation, women should be able to work with, but not be subservient to, men in physical education, athletic directors, and other department heads on campus, as well as deans and presidents. Homans planned to address this problem through BNSG's educational experiences.

The second difficulty was the discipline itself. Some older faculty members, parents, and even townspeople questioned the advisability of women entering physical education. While improving women's health through exercise appeared to be commendable, exercise during menstruation, strenuous exercise, and sport remained controversial. Some people even objected to women changing from their street dresses to less restrictive costumes for exercise classes.

There was also the lurking fear that women who liked exercise and sport might appear to have or be considered to have some masculine traits. Because Homans' students were women who exercised and participated in sports, she circumvented the possibility of such accusations with an overriding emphasis on correct feminine decorum, well-modulated voices, and faultless feminine grooming. Homans demanded that her women students be "ladies" at all times—in the classroom, in the gymnasium, in the corridors, in her office, at social receptions, and on all other occasions.

Reviewing her own life and looking ahead, Homans understood the risks she was taking and asking her students to take. If any student failed, Homans failed. It was a responsibility from which many women in the 1880s would have turned away, but Homans embraced the challenge. She accepted the role of providing the best education available in physical education, of furnishing the finest gymnasium and equipment for her school, and of eliminating in each student "as far as possible any traits or habits which would militate against success."[4] She foresaw that women, isolated in positions on faraway campuses, might be lonely and prepared her students for their professional lives by instilling in them a rare combination of professional dedication, executive ability, womanly behavior, and a loyalty to BNSG and to herself.

This approach to professional education for women made Homans a power in the lives of her students, a power of which they stood in awe, but accepted and respected. One student later wrote that the thought, "What would Miss Homans say?" became part of her conscience. Another observed, "Graduates of her School [sic] have carried with them her high ideals. Other schools of physical education, especially in the east, have had to follow the pattern she set."[5]

Homans' preparation for her new position differed from that of other physical educators of the period. Unlike Hitchcock, Sargent, Anderson, and Hartwell, Homans did not hold a medical degree but, from her point of view, such a degree was unnecessary. She had no intention of prescribing exercises or teaching classes. Her years in teaching and administration had trained her to be an administrator. She would select the faculty, admit the students, supervise the curriculum, and oversee the gymnasiums and classrooms. For this position, management and business skills and the ability to know and assess people would be needed, not a medical degree. Also, unlike Sargent, Anderson, and Allen, for whom training teachers was one of many responsibilities, Homans would focus her attention solely on education. Four basic principles appear to have guided Homans in her administration of BNSG.

First, by precept, lectures, and endless conversations she inculcated in her students the mission of BNSG and the importance of the students in that mission. A student in the early years recalls that Homans:

Saw the possibilities with a long-range view, and from the beginning directed her effort toward the goal, then decades distant, when the training and the education of the body should be as much a matter of course, as scientific, and as highly respected, as that of the mind which must use it as an instrument. . . . One of Miss Homans' greatest achievements was to see the outcome in advance and so to present it to her students that they have been able to help in its realization.[6]

Second, future teachers and administrators should master their subject matter. For BNSG students this meant a thorough grounding in the basic sciences and pedagogy, as well as Swedish gymnastics. Toward this goal, Homans planned to appoint the best faculty she could find and to secure or create the finest gymnasium facilities possible.

Third, and critical to the future of BNSG, Homans intended her students to be at ease with college presidents, deans, and other administrators; to know basic business and administrative techniques; and to be able to garner support for new programs such as exercise for women. An important facet of this third principle was that BNSG graduates must feel equal to other faculty members, most of whom would be men. Throughout her career, Homans held social functions which the students attended and where they learned to deport themselves properly under her watchful eye.

Fourth, and finally, Homans planned to place her students in positions designed to spread physical education for women across the country. Homans knew each student and had an unerring sense of the type of position in which each would do well. When a former student was ready, Homans selected her initial position, and later succeeding positions until the student was placed in a suitable permanent position, frequently as a director or administrator. In actuality, Homans instituted an administrative technique which today is called networking and which Homans utilized in the late-nineteenth century.

When the Boston Normal School of Gymnastics opened in 1889, Homans moved quickly toward her goals. Her sparse, efficient office created a strictly professional atmosphere. With a touch of immaculate white lace at her throat, she wore the dark colors of the businesswoman of the day, carried herself erectly, and displayed a firm, considered concern for every detail of the school. In dress, deportment, and the conduct of the school, she acted as a professional model for BNSG women.

In 1890 BNSG moved from the rooms on Park Street to larger quarters in the Paine Memorial Building. Located at 9 Appleton Street between Tremont and Berkely, it was accessible by

Section of gymnasium, Boston Normal School of Gymnastics, 1892–1893

horsecars and steam trains from all parts of Boston and suburban towns. The gymnasium, with a stage at one end, was equipped with stall bars on either side of the room, two window ladders, climbing ropes and ladders, and other Swedish exercise apparatus. The lecture hall was furnished with adjustable chairs and desks. Etchings of Swedish pioneers in educational gymnastics hung on the walls of the director's spacious office.

The library held about 1,000 volumes which had been selected personally by Hartwell on a visit to Europe. Laboratory equipment and a French manikin provided the students with the latest materials for study. The school installed anthropometric instruments recommended by the American Association for the Advancement of Physical Education and also Demeny machines for the study of respiratory mechanisms.

Library, Boston Normal School of Gymnastics

The printed announcement of the school's second year, 1890–1891, purported to provide "the best instruction in Swedish gymnastics to be found this side of Sweden."[7] A Boston newspaper account of the school's opening noted that "The institution will be modelled as far as possible, after the Royal Central Institute at Stockholm."[8] Posse, BNSG's first director of gymnastics, had been graduated from the Royal Central Institute and had first-hand knowledge of its organization and programs. He advised Homans on her original plans, but she apparently realized that the Swedish school was not an appropriate model for a private institution in the United States. BNSG followed the model of the Royal Central Institute in two ways. First, BNSG taught only Swedish gymnastics; and second, from the beginning, BNSG combined theoretical and practical course work.

Within a few months after the school was underway, Posse clashed with Homans and left. It is not known whether Homans suggested that he leave, but the dispute ended any professional association between them. Homans next secured Claes J. Enebuske, who had a Ph.D. from the University of Lund, Sweden, to direct gymnastics. Enebuske was the first of many highly qualified faculty members who taught at BNSG. Homans initiated a rigorous academic course of study for gymnastics and physical education, and within a few years appointed faculty members from Harvard University, Harvard Medical School, and the Massachusetts Institute of Technology to teach the basic sciences and theory courses.

In 1890–1891 BNSG students attended classes 22 ½ hours per week with two hours daily practice, demonstration and recitation in Swedish gymnastics. The theoretical work for the year was divided among 136 lectures and recitations in applied anatomy and physiology and the theory of Swedish educational gymnastics, 85 lectures and recitations in systematic anatomy, physiology, and hygiene, and 50 hours of dissection and demonstration. During the next few years major changes occurred in the curriculum and faculty which further established BNSG as an institution with very high standards. For the first time in 1891–1892 the announced curriculum distinguished between the first, or junior, year and second, or senior, year. The course of instruction listed the following offerings:

JUNIOR YEAR, THEORETICAL: 100 lectures on applied anatomy, physiology, and theory of gymnastics; 70 lectures on anatomy, physiology, and hygiene; 4 lectures on anthropometry; and 8 lectures on emergencies.

JUNIOR YEAR, PRACTICAL: Daily drill in pedagogical gymnastics; daily review in pedagogical gymnastics and instruction in teaching; weekly instruction in gymnastic games; and weekly instruction in voice training.

SENIOR YEAR, THEORETICAL: 50 lectures on theory of gymnastics and art of teaching; 50 lectures on histology and pathology; semiweekly lectures and weekly conference on psychology and pedagogy.

SENIOR YEAR, PRACTICAL: 85 hours' exercise in teaching classes of children; 85 hours' drill in the technicalities of medical gymnastics; daily drill in pedagogical gymnastics; practical talks upon personal hygiene, dress, sanitation, and ventilation will be given during the year.[9]

Homans increased the faculty to teach this expanded curricula. Beginning in 1891, she appointed Josiah Royce, Ph.D., assistant professor of philosophy at Harvard University, to lecture on psychology and pedagogy. Also that year, Dr. H. P. Bowditch, dean of Harvard Medical School, taught anthropometry and Dr. W. M. Conant of the Harvard Medical School instructed in emergencies or first aid. In addition, F. C. Robertson of Trinity College gave voice training. C. O. Louis Collin became the second instructor of gymnastics, and two assistants, Margaret S. Wallace '91 and Clara Sheppard '91, completed the staff. Homans continued to maintain her practice of appointing Ph.D.s or M.D.s to teach theoretical courses.

BNSG students added general biology, chemistry, and physics to their studies in 1893–1894. The classes were taught at MIT by the Institute's faculty members. The arrangement stated:

As the result of negotiations between the Executive Committee of the Institute and Mrs. Mary Hemenway, whose large philanthropic plans have embraced the maintenance of a normal school in Boston for the training of teachers to have charge of instruction in physical culture, an agreement was entered into by which the pupils in both years of the school referred to are to receive their instruction in Physics, Chemistry, and Biology, as special students in the Institute of Technology.[10]

Edith Sears '98 recalled "The courses offered by instructors from Harvard and Technology [MIT] were never modified for the benefit of her [Homans'] students, but were maintained on the same level as those given in their respective institutions."[11] Homans made further curricular changes demonstrating her awareness of the developing field. In addition to gymnastics, the students studied dancing and sport as important aspects of physical education.

In less than five years the BNSG curriculum developed from the study of anatomy, physiology, gymnastics, and normal or practice teaching to a much more sophisticated curriculum which added biology, chemistry, physics, histology, anthropometry, psychology, and activities such as gymnastic games, dancing, and fencing. By 1896 the students studied physics and chemistry with a weekly laboratory in chemistry, learned histology and anatomy, and had been introduced to biological principles of growth, reproduction, metabolism, sensation, and reflex actions. Students used microscopes and dissected earthworms, frogs, and mammals. They studied anatomy and physiology in detail and were expected to apply anatomical, physiological, and kinesiological principles to Swedish gymnastics. Emergencies meant first aid and covered burns, "bites of reptiles," drowned and unconscious persons, bandaging, applying splints, and proper transportation. The course in symptomatology examined organic, functional, infectious, and constitutional diseases, while hygiene dealt with personal habits such as bathing, study, sleep, "dietaries," muscular exercise, and selection of clothing.

The students practiced gymnastics daily and in their senior year taught children's classes. Psychology and pedagogy introduced the students to current inquiry in psychology and applied psychology to teaching. In addition to being thoroughly grounded in gymnastics, students learned gymnastic games, dancing, and fencing, and had lessons in voice training.

In 1893 BNSG offered a stronger curriculum than the Sargent School or the Anderson School. While they had comparable course work in anatomy, physiology, and anthropometry, only BNSG included the three basic sciences—physics, chemistry, and biology—in its curriculum. All three institutions taught activities other than gymnastics, but BNSG was the one school which taught only Swedish gymnastics. Anderson's students had the benefit of Yale University professors; Sargent's students were associated with Harvard University and Sargent's Summer School; but only BNSG claimed instruction from Harvard University, Harvard Medical School, and MIT professors.

At the time of BNSG's founding, normal schools for gymnastics were in their infancy and their graduates usually taught in nearby schools or opened private gymnasiums. Although BNSG was established ostensibly to furnish teachers of gymnastics for Boston schools, Homans placed her students well beyond Boston. Of the graduates of the first class in 1891, six held positions in institutions of higher education. Three women became directors of physical education and three were selected by Homans to remain at BNSG as assistants. These first graduates went to Massachusetts, Pennsylvania, Virginia, and as far west as Wisconsin.[12]

Under Homans' leadership, BNSG achieved immediate recognition as an outstanding normal school of gymnastics. From the beginning, she insisted on excellence in basic sciences, gymnastics, and other physical activities. Lectures, commencement exercises, professional meetings, and social engagements were all part of the students' education at BNSG. Education out of the classroom became a hallmark of the Homans touch.

6

The Homans Touch: Education Out of the Classroom

During BNSG's first five years Homans became recognized as a leader in the young field of physical education and became active in professional organizations. Only Hemenway's death in 1894 marred these early years. Homans continually improved the school and rigorously weeded out unsatisfactory students. For those whom she retained, she provided a superb education both in and out of the classroom.

Homans scrutinized every detail of the school's operation. She published a pamphlet listing "Teachers," "The Building," and "Courses," and in 1891–1892, began publishing "Catalogues." The first annual catalogue announced the "Director," "Officers of Instruction," "Lecturers," and "Courses of Instruction." Beginning in 1892–1893, the catalogues displayed photographs of the library, lecture hall, and the gymnasium with and without the apparatus in place. The following year a photograph of Homans' office was added. The catalogues also included information on the library and apparatus, a list of students, a register of graduates and the positions they held, a section on "Examinations and Diplomas," and "Requirements for Admission."

BNSG's admission requirements declared that "No one will be received as a normal pupil who has not a general education equivalent to graduation from a high school. No one with organic disease or serious functional disease can be admitted."[1] Beginning in 1892–1893, students were admitted only on probation, a practice not employed at other physical education normal schools. The probation period permitted Homans to refuse admission to those students who lacked the ability to meet the school's standards or who Homans believed would not live up to the school's ideals. In the first few weeks Homans kept a careful watch of each student's records, performance, and general behavior. Faculty members could report students who were not well prepared or did not make satisfactory progress. About 50 students were admitted but at the end of the month's probation, the number had dwindled to 25. When a student was to be dismissed, Homans called her to the office, informed her of the decision, and insisted that she leave that day. There was no opportunity to incite student sympathy or beg for another chance.

The tales surrounding the dismissals during the probation period are legendary. One story concerns a student with crooked little fingers which impaired her gymnastic positions. She refused corrective surgery and was dismissed.[2] Students who survived Homans' critical eyes that first month must have believed that they were, indeed, specially selected by Homans to undertake BNSG's mission. They complied with her every suggestion and command.

Homans not only published her requirements for admission, but also set forth the standards for diplomas and certificates. The completion of the first year's program entitled students to a certificate and, at the end of the second year, diplomas were issued to students who averaged between 70 and 80 percent. Students who averaged above 80 percent were graduated with honor. Characteristically, Homans set forth an ideal as a requirement for graduation, demanding evidence that students, in all probability, would be successful.

REQUIREMENTS FOR GRADUATION

It is the sole object of the Boston Normal School of Gymnastics to promote the highest ideals of physical education. To those who, having completed the course, have fully satisfied all the requirements and have given evidence that they are likely to maintain, or carry forward, successfully, their professional work, diplomas will be awarded.[3]

At times she required students to remain for a third year. Homans believed that some students would benefit from more

experience in teaching, improving their gymnastic performance, or conquering a bad habit. One student, who bit her nails,
had her diploma withheld until, some months following graduation, she showed Homans a perfect set of nails.[4] Whether a
student entered BNSG immediately after graduating from high
school or after receiving a bachelor's degree, she left BNSG only
after Homans had declared her a mature, professional woman.

Homans taught no classes, but frequently spoke to the entire
school and often counseled students individually. Sometimes she
presented inspirational talks while, at other times, she gave
practical demonstrations. One day she set a table with a knife,
fork, spoon, and napkin and lectured on proper table manners.
Homans summoned students to her office for personal coun-
seling where sometimes she gave the student a gentle reminder
while at other times she reduced the woman to tears. She reminded students that safety pins should not hold uniforms together, that both gloves should be on before leaving the building, and that BNSG women did not sit slumped in library seats.
She continually emphasized the importance of good posture,
good deportment, and immaculate grooming.

Mottoes hung in Homans' office, in the halls, and in the
dressing rooms, reminding the students of proper actions and
right thinking. Students memorized and tried to live up to
Shakespeare's lines:

> Her voice was ever soft, gentle and low;
> An excellent thing in woman.[5]

Homans appealed to her students to be more than gymnasts, to
be well read on many subjects and to be prepared to enter the
professional world with attitudes necessary for success. She expected her students to be the epitome of womanliness in decorum and dress, whether they were playing an arduous hockey
game or lunching with a college president. She quietly im-
parted the idea that BNSG was a superior school with the highest ideals to which she expected them to aspire.

BNSG students learned to take their rigorous academic classroom and gymnasium schedules in stride. Homans considered
these experiences important, but inadequate to prepare her

students for the professional world. As carefully as she designed their academic education and corrected their dress and manners, she arranged for lectures, professional appearances, and special occasions to teach BNSG students the necessary social graces and professional behavior. Even in the early years, Homans arranged for outstanding persons to present lectures and to speak at graduation exercises. Topics of the times varied from the challenge of being pioneers in a new profession and the importance of maintaining the high place of women in society to a review of recent physiological and psychological theories. President William DeWitt Hyde of Bowdoin College, speaking in 1892 at the graduation exercises of BNSG's second class, counseled the students not to become slaves to one system of gymnastics but to become masters of anything that would promote "strong, hale, hearty, healthy, happy boys and girls." He warned them that the true meaning of physical training was not yet accepted by most communities.

It is a grand thing to be in the fight between an old and entrenched prejudice and a new and beneficent movement, not yet clothed in the armor of conventional approach. . . . You will have your share of prejudices to meet; of opposition to encounter; of unbelief to endure; and I bid you rejoice and be exceedingly glad; for only in such fires can strong characters be formed.[6]

Hyde's remarks of 1892 were reminiscent of Homans' days in Wilmington, North Carolina, when Aunt Amy Morris Bradley and her teachers faced almost identical problems with the Southern townspeople. Homans understood facing prejudice and prepared her students for such encounters.

In the second address presented at the 1892 commencement, Dr. Charles F. Folsom reviewed the health of women in the late-nineteenth century and the beginning steps taken to improve the situation. He pointed out that a major outcome of women's colleges had been the improved health of their graduates, proving the importance of physical exercise. He praised the virtue and potential of Swedish gymnastics and expressed his thankfulness that BNSG and all that it stood for had been created.[7]

On several occasions Homans took advantage of her connections with the Royal Central Institute of Gymnastics in Sweden. In 1891, to celebrate the birthday of Per Henrik Ling, the founder of Swedish gymnastics, Homans telegraphed greetings to the Central Institute. In response, the institute sent BNSG the following message: "Many thanks! Central Institute wishes you a successful future."[8] Two years later Hemenway contributed $1,000.00 to the publication of selected drawings from the collection prepared by the founder and his son, Hjalmer Ling. Of the 600 copies published, the Central Institute kept half and sent the other half to BNSG.

In 1892 Homans sought the official endorsement of the mother school. She wrote to the directors of the Institute:

We believe that now, at this stage in our program, it would be for the best interests of Swedish gymnastics in America if the Boston Normal School of Gymnastics could be inspected and criticised by an expert. I therefore, with the advice of Madam Mary Hemenway, the founder of the school venture to request of your Honorable Board, that . . . Prof. Törngren . . . may be permitted to come to Boston and give to the school the benefit of his advice. . . . [I would like] . . . the privilege of forwarding . . . a draft sufficient to meet all expenses of the proposed journey.[9]

The Central Institute's Board of Directors carefully considered the proposal and sought additional information. Consequently, the Swedish government arranged and paid for the trip, requesting Törngren not only to visit BNSG, but also to acquaint himself with other educational institutions and physical education programs in the United States. In the spring of 1893 he traveled to the United States, attended the Congress of Physical Education in Chicago, and visited educational institutions. He observed BNSG for more than two weeks, thereby fulfilling Homans' wish. Moreover, he delivered one of the addresses to the graduating class of 1893, praising BNSG's growth and development.

I am convinced that the School . . . has not only made great efforts to display the same plan of its work that is carried out by the mother school . . . it has been very successful . . . to a far more complete point than I thought possible in so short a time. . . . The rising confidence in a respectable number of schools in different parts of this wide continent shows that its [the school's] work already is appreciated from the pedagogical side.

He complimented the students on their achievements and Homans on her administrative abilities:

Such an administration demands great care from the individual who has undertaken it, and I dare say that the confidence necessary for this . . . could not be placed in worthier hands than those of Miss Homans. Only such ability and such confidence can realize such results.[10]

He concluded by praising Hemenway and her philanthropic efforts. Homans now had the public approval of the Royal Central Institute of Sweden as another proof of the success of BNSG.

The development of physical education as a new field of study also commanded Homans' attention. If she and BNSG were to be leaders in this new field, it was necessary to join and be active in physical education organizations. In 1890 Homans joined the American Association for the Advancement of Physical Education and, in 1892, became a member of its governing council. Enebuske, who had become a member in 1888, presented a paper in 1890 and remained active in the association. In 1892 Homans served on the committee to revise the constitution of AAAPE and to suggest a reorganization of the organization. Under the new plan, Boston became the national headquarters and Homans was elected as one of the nine council members.

The annual spring meeting in 1892 took place in Philadelphia at the Drexel Institute on April 7–9. Homans seized the opportunity to place BNSG's students before the only national body of physical educators. She arranged for a group to travel to Philadelphia and perform at the meeting. The program included two demonstrations—a local group of Turners performed German gymnastics and BNSG students demonstrated Swedish gymnastics. They captivated the audience with their complex exercises executed in perfect precision. James MacAlister, the president of Drexel Institute, wrote Hemenway that it was a great compliment to Drexel to send the "young ladies" to Philadelphia and that "The exhibition given by them was the feature of the meeting."[11] Homans hoped those in attendance would note the excellent performance and identify BNSG as an outstanding educational institution and a possible source of gymnastics and physical education teachers.

On May 19, 1894, BNSG presented a program at the school for the benefit of the AAAPE, demonstrating the day's order of Swedish gymnastics, a game of Corner Ball, gymnastic dancing, and basketball. Considering the year, 1894, this was a very forward-looking program. In addition to gymnastics, a game, dancing, and a sport were offered as part of an overall program of physical education. While many historians of physical education place the "play" movement and "sport" in the curriculum in the early decades of the twentieth century, Homans included both play and sport well before that time. Her early efforts in physical education associations helped mold the profession and set a pattern for BNSG graduates.

When Homans became active in AAAPE, Sargent was president. While they appeared to have been amiable on a professional level, a rivalry sprang up between the Sargent School and BNSG. In subtle ways, such as not permitting BNSG students to sit on the floor at a gymnastics performance at which Sargent students *were* seated on the floor, emphasizing BNSG's probationary period, and the school's connections with Harvard and MIT, Homans made her students aware that she considered BNSG the superior school.

Homans instilled in BNSG women the need for bachelor's degrees and then for more advanced degrees, warning them that the time would come when every woman entering the profession would be required to have at least a bachelor's degree. She urged those who did not enter the school with a degree to continue their studies as quickly as possible.

Homans displayed an uncanny ability in placing her students in positions, sensing that certain students would be particularly effective in one situation and very ineffective in another. A few, such as Margaret Wallace '91 and Ethel Perrin '92, remained at BNSG as assistants and then as faculty members. Perrin recounts that, after fourteen years at BNSG, Homans believed she should move and arranged for her to teach at Smith College for one year, and then at the University of Michigan. Following a year at Michigan, the Detroit Public School system hired Perrin at Homans' recommendation. Perrin remained in that position and became an outstanding leader in physical education.[12]

Homans constantly sought evaluations of her students in their professional positions. She wrote to H. B. Frissell at Hampton Institute, Virginia, inquiring about the performance of Lucy Pratt '95 and Jessie Coope '97, asking whether their youth was against them and if they were acceptable to other members of the faculty. She commented that the last was an important question to the development of BNSG.[13] Ever mindful of the necessity of securing good positions for her students, Homans, at the same time, concerned herself with the reputation which BNSG must maintain.

Much to Homans' personal sorrow, Mary Hemenway died on March 6, 1894, following a short illness. Newspaper accounts, associations, and friends extolled her life and her philanthropy, especially recognizing her latest efforts in physical education. One of the most touching tributes came from some of BNSG's first students:

In tender memory the members of the class look back to the time when the practical department for physical training was in its infancy, and as they note the outgrowth of this movement to keep the balance between mind and body in establishing the Boston Normal School of Gymnastics upon a firm basis, they recognize the noble hearted woman whose works do follow her.[14]

The memorial, dated April 2, 1894, was signed by twenty-five women.

Hemenway's will expressed her purposes in her philanthropic endeavors, "to promote a higher physical, intellectual, and religious life among those to be benefited, since the building up of character has been my aim in all my undertakings." Her will made explicit her wishes for the future of BNSG:

It is my will that for at least two years after my decease said Trustees shall continue to carry on the Archaeological work, the Boston Normal School of Gymnastics, and Boston Normal School of Cookery, and said work connected with the Old South Meeting House . . . in the manner, on the scale, and to the extent carried on and approved by me. . . . I will and direct that said Boston Normal School of Gymnastics shall be continued so long during all said fifteen years as said Amy M. Homans is able to direct the same.

Hemenway bequeathed to Homans $5,000.00 "in loving and grateful appreciation of her aid in the educational work I have undertaken for seventeen years."[15] She left to Homans and her sister Gertrude the use of the house at 26 Berwick Park, the trustees to pay the taxes, insurance, and repairs. After Hemenway's death, a Board of Trustees supervised the school under the terms of Hemenway's will.

For the rest of her life Homans adopted Hemenway's phrase, "in the manner, on the scale, and to the extent carried on and approved by me" as standards for herself and BNSG. Before Hemenway's death "her manner, scale, and extent" had made it possible to arrange for BNSG students to have instruction from authorities at Harvard and MIT, for Hartwell to select an excellent collection of books from European libraries for BNSG's collection, for students to attend a national meeting to demonstrate Swedish gymnastics, and to invite Törngren to the United States from Sweden to visit BNSG. Hemenway's standards for her work were high, but she firmly believed that worthy projects deserved sufficient support to be successful. Following these principles, translating "manner" into excellent professional standards, "scale" into educational advantages for her students, and "extent" into foreseeing the future of physical education, Homans resolutely sought every opportunity to make BNSG worthy of Hemenway's ideals.

BNSG's fifth annual catalogue, 1895–1896, lists 110 graduates of whom 32 taught in public and private schools and 27 in colleges, normal schools, and institutes. Sixteen engaged in private practice, five were employed in YWCAs, and several in special institutions such as reformatories and asylums. Helen Woods '91 enrolled in the Medical College in Philadelphia and Maude Hopkins, also '91, was the director of physical training for women at Drexel Institute in that same city. Helen Rogers '93 held the position of director of public schools in Lynn, Massachusetts, while Mary Elizabeth Bates '93 taught at Bryn Mawr College and Senda Berenson '92 had been appointed director of physical training at Smith College. The director of physical training at the Normal and Industrial College in Milledgeville, Georgia, was Sarah Boudren '93 and a classmate, Sarah Jacobs '93, was an instructor of gymnastics at the State Normal School in Los Angeles, California. Lillian Curtis Drew '93 assisted Dr. E. H. Bradford in Boston and Emma Babcock '95 was the director of physical training at the YWCA in Dayton, Ohio.[16] Homans placed her students in public schools, women's colleges, state normal schools, as assistants to medical doctors such as Dr. Bradford, in charge of YWCA programs, and in institutions for special populations. In BNSG's first years Homans had begun her unique approach to professional education for women, providing leaders who would influence and develop women's physical education in the coming decades.

7

From Gymnastic Teachers to Gymnasium Directors: Toward a Profession for Women

As the nineteenth century drew to a close, BNSG had become recognized as a first-rate educational institution and Homans had taken her place among the outstanding physical educators of the day. By this time, the lives of women had somewhat changed in ways which would affect the future of women in physical education. Increasing numbers volunteered their services for suffrage campaigns, settlement house work, civic clubs, and other reform movements which they thought would better the country. Thousands joined the work force, some from economic necessity and others filling time while they waited for marriage. Higher education for women appeared to be more widely accepted and the importance of exercise in maintaining college women's vigor was better understood. Some progress had been made in beginning exercise programs in high schools and elementary schools. Among their new interests, many women enjoyed recreational sports and pastimes such as roller skating, horseback riding, and bicycling. An amateur championship for women in tennis began in 1887 and in golf in 1895. Basketball and field hockey became the rage among the many games popular with college women.

In spite of these new freedoms, many critics continued to frown on higher education and physical activity for women, especially sport. G. Stanley Hall compiled statistics showing that college graduates had fewer children then noncollege graduates. The American interpretation of Freud's new psychological theories also reinforced the perspective of women as inferior, passive, emotional, and dependent. Other critics questioned whether sport, which encouraged aggressive, active, and independent qualities, made women "masculine." Even Sargent, who championed developing a woman's "body, limbs, and vital organism," did not recommend "exercises that, when pushed to extremes, tend to unsex her." He referred to highly competitive games and sports and cautioned that women playing men's games under men's rules might acquire masculine characteristics.[1]

While Homans and other leaders in physical education had made some headway in overcoming prejudices against women in physical education and sport, clearly much remained to be done. Homans developed BNSG into a model school that emphasized the feminine qualities of exercise and sport and the "womanliness" of BNSG graduates. She continued to strengthen BNSG, moving the school to larger quarters, making curriculum changes, introducing sport, adding courses such as playground management, and, as always, insisting on correct womanly deportment in and out of class. She initiated professional and alumnae activities, realizing that they were essential to her plans to develop a profession of physical education for women.

In 1897 the school moved from Appleton Street to the Massachusetts Charitable Mechanics Association on Huntington Avenue near Exeter Street. The new school provided substantially improved quarters. The gymnasium occupied about 4,000 square feet and included an auditorium. It was equipped not only with all the necessary Swedish apparatus, but also with basketball backboards and baskets. In addition to the main gymnasium, there were rooms for special uses—lecture rooms, an anthropometric room, and another for corrective exercises. The ample dressing room accommodations, boasting shower and needle baths, were located on the same floor as the gymnasium, an amazing innovation in the 1890s. As always, Homans paid special attention to the library resources for the school. Students could study in the library from nine o'clock in the morning until six at night. The spacious, sunny room was furnished with arm chairs and study tables and had "a card catalogue and a generous supply of periodical reading, both professional and literary," offering "one of the most stimulating influences in the school year."[2] Library additions increased the holdings to about 1,200 in 1901–1902. By 1899 the school had acquired 40 microscopes, mounted and disarticulated skeletons, a large number of anatomical charts, and a life-size Auzoux model of the human body.[3]

Prospective students and their families could learn a great deal about BNSG from the annual catalogues. They described in detail the school, the facilities, and the curriculum, showing a block schedule for each year's program. They included information about the Alumnae Loan Fund, available to second year students, and the "Register of Graduates," giving each student's present position, which suggested the employment prospects for interested applicants. Beginning in 1903–1904, the catalogue listed the pamphlets, papers, and other materials published by the school.

Homans continued to refine the admission procedures and, by 1901, the school included written and spoken English in its requirements. The following year the catalogue added an application blank which requested references as well as information about the student's physical condition, educational advantages, and experience in physical training and teaching. The general education requirement had to be equivalent to "that required for graduation from the full (four-year) course of a high school." Applicants "must in addition submit a written statement from the principal of the school last attended attesting the applicant's graduation, the subjects studied, and the character of the work done in each subject."[4] The 1906–1907 admission requirements added a "keen sense of rhythm."[5]

Recognizing the potential of physical education and the future needs of her students, Homans greatly expanded the curriculum. She never swerved from her beliefs that courses in the foundation sciences were essential and that professional education should follow a liberal arts education. She moved steadily away from the focus on Swedish gymnastics to a wide range of physical activities. The introduction, in 1899–1900, of a course in kinesiology in the junior year and corrective gymnastics in the senior year indicated the trend toward the science of movement as the basis for physical education. Beginning in 1901 physics and chemistry were offered in the junior year. If a student had had these subjects in college, she could be exempt if the instructor approved her laboratory notebook.

A two-year course combining biology and hygiene covered the phenomena of life and problems of health. The first year of the course included gross anatomy, skeletal and muscular, a study of the major organs of the body and their functions, the systematic dissection of a mammal, cellular structures, and the foundations of animal physiology. "A large amount of reading is encouraged, designed to convey to the student the scope and interrelation of biological subjects. Locy's 'Biology and its Makers' is prescribed for outside biographical reading. The course closes with a discussion of the Theory of Descent."[6] In its second year the course covered theoretical physiology, the study of the scientific method, and experiments in reflex action. Each student prepared a paper on topics such as "The Mechanism of Heat Regulation," "The Vaso-motor Mechanism," "Environment and Pre-natal Development," and "The Relation of Structure to Function in Striated Muscle." Finally, the course synthesized biological and hygienic principles toward understanding "the responsibility of the individual to himself and to the race, and the higher worth in the balance and rhythm of perfect bodily adaptation."[7]

The students also studied applied anatomy, paying special attention to the skeleton and joint articulations. Through the discussion of the progression, selection, and arrangement of exercises in the gymnastic lesson, the course provided the basis for the senior year course in the theory of gymnastics and the art of teaching. The seniors visited nearby gymnasiums, schools, and playgrounds, and did practice teaching at BNSG and Chelsea public schools. Practical experience in corrective gymnastics was gained at Boston's Children's Hospital.

Other courses in the curriculum included a short course on symptomatology which enabled BNSG students to detect conditions in their students which might require the attention of a physician and to work more intelligently with physicians in the treatment of students. In Royce's course, "Psychology and Pedagogy," the students examined the theory and practice of teaching.

The purpose of the course . . . is: (1) to give some idea of the principal elementary results of modern psychological inquiry; (2) to cultivate in the members of the class such an interest in the study of mental life and such habits of psychological observation and analysis as will be of most service in the work of the practical teacher; (3) to give as clear an idea as is possible, within the limited time, of the application of psychology to the actual business of teaching. In addition to the lectures, the class will be expected to cultivate and to show, by a limited amount of written work, their power to apply the instruction given to the actual study of mental processes in themselves, or in their pupils.[8]

By 1908–1909 students studied the history and literature of physical education. The course purported "to give the student a connected outline of the rise and development of physical education as a science," and "to emphasize the relation of the physical director to the movement for national health today."[9]

Well ahead of the times, Homans introduced dance and sport activities in the curriculum. In 1898–1899 the purpose of the school stated that "thorough and scientific instruction is provided, not only in the Ling, or Swedish, system of gymnastics, but also in those general principles of physiology, psychology, and the hygiene of the human body, upon which sound physical training must also depend."[10] The next year "games" and "dancing" were listed after gymnastics; then, in 1901–1902, "athletics"; in 1902–1903, "swimming"; and in 1903–1904, "fencing".[11] By 1908 BNSG students not only performed gymnastic exercises and directed corrective gymnastics, but also danced, folk danced, fenced, swam, ran races, jumped hurdles, paddled canoes, and played tennis, basketball, and field hockey. The term "physical training" had been replaced by "physical education," which included a broad program of physical activities organized as part of the overall educational experience. Homans foresaw the potential for the rapidly growing field of physical education for women and realized that these new activities would be incorporated in future programs.

Dancing, first introduced as part of a course in games and dancing, became a separate course in 1898 when Homans appointed Melvin Ballou Gilbert as instructor in aesthetic dancing. "Gilbert Dancing," which combined social and ballet tech-

Class of 1906 playing field hockey at Riverside Recreation Grounds

BNSG, Rhythmical gymnastics, c. 1906

niques, became popular after it was introduced in 1893 at the Harvard Summer School of Physical Education. Gilbert created his dance forms while teaching in Portland, Maine, and in 1897 moved to Boston where he opened the Gilbert Normal School of Dancing. The 1899 Catalogue described dancing as "applied gymnastics":

In which the power of co-ordination and the sense of rhythm are especially trained. The movements are more complicated, less localized, less sharply defined, than formal gymnastic exercises. They are continuous, rhythmical, and of constantly varying character, involving blended but partial action of a great number of joints and muscles rather than powerful, complete action of a few. The practical results obtained are grace and ease of movement and bearing as well as a considerable amount of endurance.[12]

Homans again seized the opportunity to offer the latest in physical activities and appointed Gilbert himself as the instructor. By 1902 the term *classic* dance replaced *aesthetic* dance in the catalogue but the description remained the same. A course in folk-dancing was added in 1908–1909, indicating Homans' awareness of the growing interest in ethnic dancing and the importance of learning a variety of physical activities.

The Brookline Public Baths, a swimming facility in a nearby suburb, opened in 1897. Homans arranged for BNSG students to have swimming instruction that fall. Although Oberlin, Vassar, Smith, and Bryn Mawr had small swimming pools or "baths," most educational institutions did not yet have swimming facilities. Homans, however, placed her students in many positions other than in educational institutions and, looking ahead, she anticipated an increased interest in aquatic activities.

In keeping with Homans' overriding concern to mold exercise and sport into acceptable activities for women, the course in athletics at first offered only lectures on the subject, but, three years later, introduced a limited amount of practice. The course familiarized the students with methods of training for and management of field and track athletics in schools and colleges, and enabled them, if called upon, to organize such sports in boys' schools, and more particularly to give them some basis for their introduction, in modified form, into girls' schools and colleges. Discussions of the relation of athletics to physical education in general, of the rules governing intercollegiate athletic contests, of sample schedules of training for the different events of such contests, and of the management of athletics meets are supplemented by demonstrations and a limited amount of practice of the different games in the gymnasium as well as by an informal indoor meet.[13]

Although the activity permitted in the course would be considered minimal today, Homans insisted that her students be acquainted with the changing nature of physical education activities. The description of the course suggests that Homans expected to place her students in positions where they might supervise young men. Homans, ever aware of physical education within the larger picture of society in general, moved ahead of most physical educators, who, at their 1899 national meeting, still argued over the place of games and play in physical education.[14]

Another major innovation in 1901–1902 was the use of the Riverside Recreation Grounds for individual and team sports. Ladylike, clad in long skirts, BNSG women traveled on the trolley car to the playing fields. Tennis, field hockey, and basketball are listed in the catalogue, followed by "etc.," indicating that more sports might have been offered. Students recall boating and canoeing as well. The well-known English field hockey coach, Constance M. K. Applebee, taught at BNSG from 1902 to 1904. During these years Applebee toured the Eastern women's colleges promoting the game in the United States. Again, Applebee's appointment demonstrates Homans' forward approach to the curriculum and her ability to attract the best possible faculty to her school.

Homans responded to the growing concern over the supervision of city children by instituting a course on playground supervision. The movement to oversee the play of city children in crowded neighborhoods began in 1885 when the Massachusetts Emergency and Hygiene Association provided "sand gardens" for Boston's young children. The founding of the Playground

Association of America in 1906 demonstrated the growing national concern for children's activities. Just two years later Homans introduced the study of play and playgrounds, emphasizing the theory of play, the classification of pupils for activities, and the adaptation of playgrounds for all-year use. According to the catalogue, "This course is intended to fit students for playground work, and will enable them to act as superintendents, principals, and instructors."[15] Even in the course description, Homans indicated her intention that her students would be the administrators and not the playground supervisors.

As always, the students, as well as the curriculum, commanded Homans' attention. Probations continued to be a reality. Mabel Lee '10 relates that she burst into tears in an early encounter with Homans, who threatened her with dismissal if she failed to gain ten pounds during the probationary period. Lee gained the weight while learning to comply with Homans' wishes, became stronger and enjoyed a sense of well-being.[16] Another member of the same class, Lucile Grunewald '10 from Chicago, having heard tales of Homans' standards, arrived in Boston with a certain amount of trepidation. During her initial physical examination her heart raced to such an extent that her admission was questionable. However, Homans asked her to have it rechecked in several days. At that time Grunewald was considerably calmer and was admitted to the school.[17]

Homans' relentless campaign for perfection in her students is well remembered by graduates at the turn of the century. Winifred Van Hagen '04 recalled her summons to Homans' office where she was greeted graciously. After a few remarks, Homans asked her if she was aware that she walked like a sailor. "You know," said Homans, "Miss Van Hagen, you *roll*." Van Hagen admitted that she was not aware that she "rolled" and, under Homans' direction, walked up and down the office correcting her walk until Homans dismissed her, apparently satisfied that Van Hagen no longer walked like a sailor.[18]

Invitations to lunch with Homans, usually at Boston's Parker House or Hotel Brunswick, brought yet another test. Homans sometimes ordered complicated dishes requiring careful handling and then supervised the proper use of cutlery. Students also learned proper visiting etiquette. They were invited to bring a friend and visit Homans at her Boston home. If they found Homans not at home, they were instructed to leave their calling cards. Marion Mention Hamilton '04 dreaded the experience, but bolstered and accompanied by her friend, John Hamilton, mustered her courage to make the expected call. A uniformed maid opened the door and informed the young couple that Homans was not in, and accepted the calling card. Years later, Marion Hamilton described their relief on not having to make that formal call: "We waited until the maid shut the door, turned, threw our hats in the air, raced down the steps and dashed off for our own good time."[19]

With all Homans' attention to both the professional and social preparation of her students, she also concerned herself with their personal welfare and happiness. Because she thought Sarah Davis '07 somewhat provincial, she made sure that she was included in social functions.[20] In another instance Homans quietly reminded Fanny Garrison '03 to include a black student in games. When the black student was to be a guest at a hotel, Homans contacted the hotel to be sure she would be received graciously. While the North was theoretically not segregated at that time, many hotels did not welcome black guests.[21] On another occasion Homans learned that a student planned to stay at home from a school function because she did not have an appropriate dress. Homans went with the girl to examine the dresses in her wardrobe. She pointed out to the student that she, Homans, would be wearing a black dress several years old and that the girl had a lovely dress in a becoming color not nearly as old as Homans' dress.[22]

Quite a different situation occurred in one of the boarding houses where the students lived. Winifred Van Hagen '04 had a serious misunderstanding with the rooming house owner who falsely accused her of misbehaving. Van Hagen reported the incident to Homans who removed all the students from the house that day.[23] Many students lived in Rutland Square at Miss Blake's boarding house. In 1909 Homans arranged for a group of students who would be unable to go home for spring vacation to visit Miss Blake's second home in Gloucester, just north of Boston, where the women enjoyed a pleasant vacation. On occasion, Homans requested students to walk with her, perhaps to enjoy the walk or to get to know them better. Marion Watters Babcock '10 remembered the flurry of excitement when Homans stopped at Rutland Square to invite Izzie (Isabel Dowell '09) and her to go walking. They walked through the Fens toward Harvard, returned by trolley, and reported a fine outing.[24]

Typical of all students, the women made their own good times. Diaries tell of fudge parties and trips to local theaters where, for 25 cents, the students could sit in the high gallery. And like every school, BNSG had a school song:

> Oh B.N.S.G., dearly we love thee;
> Our hearts are filled with glorious pride
> When to bear with us you do decide.
>
> Your name shines out in gold
> O'er land and sea we're told.
>
> We know that wherever we may be
> We will always love B.N.S.G.
>
> Oh B. N. S. G.
> *Dearly we* love *thee*.[25]

For the BNSG student, life combined serious study, learning to meet Homans' qualifications of "womanliness," and moments of relaxation and fun.

These moments never overshadowed the professional programs, lectures, and social events which Homans arranged for the students. In 1904 Theodore Hough of MIT, who taught physiology to BNSG students, was made president of the American Society for Research in Physical Education. G. W. Fitz of Harvard was made secretary. BNSG hosted a 1904 meeting where papers were presented on the curvature of the spine, respiratory functions, the influence of practice on muscular contraction, and a new form of pantograph for body tracing.[26] In 1907 the New England Education League met at BNSG to discuss the increasing recognition of physical education in secondary schools and colleges. Chaired by President F. W. Hamilton of Tufts College, the conferees, including Hill of Wellesley College, Sedgwick of MIT, Sargent of Harvard, and Homans deliberated on the subjects to be included under physical training and whether or not physical training should rank as a major subject in high schools and colleges.[27] In 1896–1897 William H. Burnham of Clark University, Jakob Bolin of New York, and Dr. Robert Lovett of Boston spoke to the students. Dr. R. Tait McKenzie, medical director of physical training and demonstrator of anatomy at McGill University, lectured on "Expressions of the Emotions by the Face" in 1901–1902. Also that year Dr. Edward Waldo Emerson delivered two lectures, "The Relation of Animal Structure to Art" and "The Relation of Art to Life." William James spoke on "The Gospel of Relaxation," stressing the importance of releasing emotions that inhibit effective and creative living.

What our girl-students and woman-teachers most need nowadays is not the exacerbation, but rather the toning-down of their moral tensions. Even now I fear that some one of my fair hearers may be making an undying resolve to become strenuously relaxed, cost what it will, for the remainder of her life.

He cautioned them to "*Unclamp . . .* your intellectual and practical machinery, and let it run free; and the service it will do you will be twice as good."[28] Following the lectures, receptions were held to permit the students to meet these well-known authorities and, at the same time, gain social confidence. Marion Watters Babcock '10 recalled that when Homans asked her if she would like to meet Professor James she answered that she would and started to follow Homans. Homans turned to her and said, "My dear, if a lady is to meet a gentleman, she remains seated and he is brought to her."[29]

The Alumnae Association heard Clarence J. Blake in 1905 on "The Spirit of a Profession" in which he traced the intellectual awakening of women in the nineteenth century and the development of women in trades and professions. Blake distinguished between a trade as an occupation which queries, "What can I get?" and a profession which asks, "What can I give?" On this basis he justified physical education as a profession. Completely in keeping with the social beliefs of the early twentieth century and in the context of Homans' ideals of womanliness, Blake reminded his audience that they possessed "initial sympathies, [an] . . . innate desire to help and protect." He likened the body to a temple of the soul and the physical education teacher to the keeper of the temple. "The influence for good of an honest, sincere, and helpful-minded woman, able to use her mental processes intelligently, is incalculable." He suggested that home-making was frequently more demanding than teaching, but for those who continued to teach their task was home-sharing. He concluded "there must be always, illuminating your own lives, that light, which makes clear the spirit of your profession,—the light of an educated appreciation of normal uses, the spirit which carries you beyond yourselves into the lives of others."[30]

Blake's analysis of a profession distinguished between work for which one is paid and service to the community for which one receives a salary, but which one enters not for the sake of money alone, but to contribute to the betterment of the community. His stress on womanly qualities reflected the current views of women as the moral reformers of society. While Homans agreed that women had a place as reformers, she did not agree with society's views of educated women leaders as passive, emotional, and dependent. These characteristics would not prepare her students to take their place in a professional world where they would be in the vanguard. She intended her students, who had an excellent academic and social background, to conduct physical education programs in colleges, schools, and social agencies. In such positions, they would be required to be active, not passive; rational, not emotional; and independent— able to form their own opinions and make decisions—not dependent. Again, Homans' educational philosophy is known to us, not from her writings, but from her students and their professional lives.

By this time, Homans distinguished between physical education for women and for men. While both men and women should study the foundational sciences, she believed that gymnastics, dance, and sport programs differed for men and women. She appeared to agree with the general social beliefs of the period that women should not play all team games and sports in the

identical manner as men. By modifying sports and creating rules
for women, sport and physical education for women became a
separate entity, not to be identified with rough, body-contact
sports such as football.

She agreed with Blake that physical education was a profession and, by now, had clearly formulated her plans for physical
education for women. Looking back from today's sociological
analysis of a profession, Homans' framework of physical education for women had emerged. She increasingly explained her
purpose in terms of preparing women for a profession. For
Homans, physical education for women should improve the
physical, mental, emotional, and social well-being of women,
thereby improving the health of future generations. She fur-
thered knowledge in the support of physical education. She appointed faculty who undertook research and often published
their work. Homans took the lead in curricular changes and instituted dance and sport activities to supplement gymnastics. She
began to create a cohesive group of women with identifiable
qualifications, attitudes, and ethical behaviors associated with her
high ideals.

Homans encouraged her students and alumnae to be loyal to
BNSG and thus to her. As the number of the alumnae grew,
they became an early-twentieth century women's network. By
1906, 369 students had been graduated from BNSG. The
members of the pioneer class of 1891 were probably in their
mid-thirties in 1906 and, as a group, the BNSG alumnae were
very young. While many married, most engaged in some aspect
of physical education. A number directed physical education in
public schools and YWCAs and worked in corrective gymnastics with private physicians. The nucleus of leaders in physical
education for women were faculty members in institutions of
higher learning. Positions were held in colleges, universities, or
normal schools by 60 women and, of these, 26 were directors
of physical education.[31] They also assumed leadership when it
became necessary to institute control of women's sport. When
the first women's basketball committee of four women was appointed in 1889, three of those women were graduates of BNSG.

While Homans maneuvered physical education for women
toward a recognizable profession and placed her students in

positions of leadership, the future of BNSG was in doubt. By the terms of Hemenway's will, funds with which to conduct the school were provided until 1909. By then, Hemenway had expected BNSG to merge with a four-year liberal arts college. Homans believed that, in the future, all physical education teachers should hold at least a bachelor's degree, and she also saw the need for teacher training programs to train others to teach. The directors of such programs or departments of physical education for women should have work beyond the bachelor's degree. The need would be not so much for a two-year normal course which trained gymnastics, dance, and sport teachers, but for a graduate program which accepted students with a bachelor's degree and prepared them for administrative positions to develop programs and train others to teach. Finding an academic institution which would serve her purpose created a crisis in Homans' life and the future of BNSG.

8

The Crisis in Homans' Plans

As early as 1903, the BNSG trustees began to make arrangements for the future of the school. While some correspondence exists between Homans and the trustees on the future of BNSG, more discussions and considerations must have taken place. As far as is known, only universities and colleges in the Boston area were considered. Homans, with her exceptionally high academic standards and her plans for the future of BNSG and the profession of physical education for women, did not find the local physical education normal schools acceptable.

Theoretically, BNSG might have merged with Sargent's or Posse's school. It might appear that an affiliation with Sargent and Harvard would appeal to Homans. In 1902 Sargent added to his course a third year and a summer camp term in New Hampshire. The school moved to a new gymnasium in 1904 and, to outward appearances, the combination of Sargent and BNSG would have created an unusually fine school. However, there are many indications that the two leaders often disagreed on professional matters and Homans intimated in many small ways that she considered BNSG superior to Sargent's school. An affiliation with Sargent probably would mean losing BNSG's identity and Homans' position, both of which would be unacceptable to Homans. Posse, BNSG's first gymnastic director who left the school during its first year, opened his own normal school. After his death in 1895, his wife, an American with no professional training other than her work with Posse, became the director of the school. Homans probably believed that

BNSG's status would not be enhanced by an affiliation with Posse.

The possibility of locating the school at State Normal School at Framingham, where the Boston Normal School of Cookery had been transferred after Hemenway's death, appears not to have been considered. Again, it can be posited that Homans had higher hopes for her program than a state teacher-training institution. Other institutions educating women in the Boston area at that time were Wellesley College, Boston University with its theological program, Tufts University which first admitted women in 1892, and Simmons College, founded from the estate of John Simmons for the purpose of educating women for specific vocations or careers. There is no record that Homans investigated each of these institutions as a possible location for BNSG. The BNSG trustees, two of whom had connections with Simmons College, began negotiations with Simmons in the hopes that it would accept BNSG. At some point during the period of negotiations with Simmons, Homans approached Wellesley College with a proposal for affiliation.

Simmons College seemed an excellent choice. Augustus Hemenway, Mary Hemenway's son and a BNSG trustee, became the first president of the Simmons governing corporation. Horatio Lamb, another BNSG trustee, followed Hemenway after a year. When Simmons opened in 1902 it was located near BNSG and Simmons students took gymnastics twice a week at BNSG. In 1904 it moved to the Fenway, occupying a building which lacked a gymnasium.[1] The suggestion that the BNSG trustees provide Simmons with a gymnasium and that Simmons accept BNSG seemed to meet the needs of both Simmons and BNSG.

Although negotiations with Simmons began in 1903, no decision had been reached by 1906. The trustees insisted that Homans announce the possible discontinuance of BNSG at least two years prior to the actual date and, to this end, they prepared a statement for publication in the school's catalogue. Homans objected to their statement, but finally agreed to the following notice which appeared in the 1906–1907 *Catalogue*:

Mrs. Mary Hemenway, who died in 1894, made provision in her will for carrying on the Boston Normal School of Gymnastics for fifteen years.

The School is so eminently successful, and is doing such important work for education, that the Trustees are very desirous that a sufficient endowment to secure its permanence be obtained. As up to the present time, however, this has not been accomplished, they think it their duty to call attention to the terms of Mrs. Hemenway's will, and to say that a decision relative to the continuance of the School after June, 1909, will be reached, and announced not later than January 1, 1908.[2]

To make such a public announcement of BNSG's uncertain future must have been personally difficult for Homans. By this time BNSG commanded great respect from professional colleagues, as well as from presidents and deans who employed BNSG graduates.

Sometime before June, 1906, the BNSG trustees approached Simmons, offering $50,000.00 toward the construction of a building for the Boston Normal School of Gymnastics and an additional sum of $50,000.00 for a trust fund, the income of which would help defray the expenses of maintaining BNSG's program. In return, Simmons College students could expect to use the gymnasium when the BNSG students were not using it. The Simmons corporation "did not deem it wise" to accept this offer because of the inadequate funds, suggesting that at least $150,000.00 was necessary for a building and a similar sum would be required for maintaining the program. The BNSG trustees withdrew their offer but, in case the Simmons corporation changed its mind, agreed not to approach another institution until October, 1907.[3] Simmons continued to study the matter and, in November, approached Andrew Carnegie with the hope that he would give the school a gymnasium. The college would then accept $100,000.00 from the BNSG trustees to continue the school. Simmons failed in its efforts to obtain a building from Carnegie,[4] and the BNSG trustees suggested that Homans approach Carnegie, officers of the Sage Foundation, or other appropriate persons who might donate a gymnasium.[5] The trustees emphasized to Homans that the gymnasium must be a gift to Simmons and not to BNSG, because BNSG did not have sufficient resources to continue in its present form. It is clear that the BNSG trustees had agreed that, if a satisfactory affiliation could not be arranged, the school would close.[6] Homans failed in her attempts to obtain a donor but, by this time, she had hopes that Wellesley College would accept the school. Located just thirteen miles west of Boston, situated on beautiful, extensive grounds bordering Lake Waban, the college needed a gymnasium.

Wellesley's founder, Henry Fowle Durant, believed that physical exercise and recreation developed and maintained the vigor necessary to withstand the perils of college life and academic work. He appointed an instructor in gymnastics and a woman physician to live at the college and consult with students on matters of health. The small gymnasium, built in the 1870s, was outmoded. As far back as 1899, President Hazard had declared the gymnasium unsuitable.[7] The campus had ample land for a gymnasium and playing fields which would meet the needs of both Wellesley students and a professional program in physical education.

Wellesley's strong liberal arts undergraduate curriculum and its graduate programs certainly must have attracted Homans. There were both disadvantages and advantages to consider in affiliating with Wellesley. A merger with Wellesley would mean severing instructional contacts with Harvard, MIT, and local hospitals. On the other hand, Wellesley's excellent faculty would be available for basic subjects such as English and foundation sciences such as chemistry and physics. Visits to Boston's hospitals could be arranged and Harvard and MIT professors could visit Wellesley for special lectures. If a merger took place, Homans would see her beloved program affiliated with a first-rate undergraduate liberal arts college and, in return, BNSG would provide a gymnasium for the undergraduate students and an endowment fund for the conduct of the professional program in physical education. Further, Wellesley offered graduate study and, in this regard, would make Homans' plans for the future of physical education for women possible.

Before October 30, 1907, Homans met with several trustees of Wellesley to explore the possibilities of BNSG moving to Wellesley. The language of a letter sent to Homans from the BNSG trustees suggests that it is a letter of confirmation rather than a letter of inquiry:

The trustees would be glad to give Wellesley College the sum of $100,000 as a trust fund substantially under the following conditions . . . the college must receive and manage this sum as a separate fund and apply the income towards the continuance of the work of the school substantially as it is at present or as it may grow to be in natural development; but if the college gives up the work of the school or substantially changes it, then it must give over the fund with its increase or diminution to some other charity in which Mrs. Hemenway was interested to be named by us in the deed of trust. As to the conditions, the trustees will give this sum to the college only on the condition that you raise before Jan. 1, 1908, directly or indirectly, an additional sum of $200,000 to be given to the college to carry on the work of the school including the erection of a gymnasium suitable and adequate for such work.[8]

The experience with Simmons possibly led the trustees to name such a large sum, or perhaps Homans had talked with an architect and now knew the amount of money required to build an ideal gymnasium. With the full cooperation of Wellesley's President Hazard, Homans undertook raising the funds, but found it an impossible task. Hazard also helped by seeking $150,000.00 from the General Education Board. On December 3, 1907, Homans wrote to H. B. Frissell at Hampton Institute, a member of the board whom she knew, attempting to enlist his support in the matter. She outlined the situation to him, accounting for the $200,000.00 with a grant from the General Education Board and the rest from the alumnae, even though they were fewer than 400. Homans explained that about a half million dollars of Hemenway money already had been invested in BNSG and that the money had certainly been well used. She stressed the importance of the work done at BNSG and that the school had an international reputation. She pointed out the importance of good facilities and a good hygiene program for the Wellesley undergraduates. Frissell forwarded Homans' letter to Dr. Wallace Buttrick, secretary of the General Education Board, and promised to talk to him personally about the matter.[9]

Learning that the General Education Board did not meet until January 31, 1908, the trustees extended Homans' deadline from January 1 to February 15. Homans again requested more

time.[10] Homans' and Wellesley's pleas to the General Education
Board, Carnegie, and Sage for a gymnasium were unsuccessful,
and by March, Homans realized that her original hopes for an
ideal gymnasium might not materialize. Homans' frantic and
unsuccessful efforts during the early months of 1908 led to re-
ducing the original goal of $200,000.00 for a gymnasium to
$100,000.00, suggesting a temporary structure, if necessary.[11]
Meanwhile, Wellesley seemed inclined to accept the BNSG
trustees' offer, even though the building fund was incomplete.
Negotiations had advanced sufficiently to mention the possible
affiliation with Wellesley College in the next BNSG catalogue.
"The trustees cannot as yet speak definitively about the continuance of the School, but they have good reason to believe that
Wellesley College will, on the expiration of the trust, carry on
the work with an endowment fund."[12]

There is no suggestion that the tenuous state of the school in
any way affected BNSG's ability to attract able students. The
faculty and all the school's programs proceeded as if BNSG
would continue in its present form. During this time, Homans
kept trying, but in vain, to raise the money for a gymnasium.
As Hazard pointed out, "Miss Homans thinks she can raise this
money; but, poor lady, she thought she could raise the whole
one hundred thousand dollars, and she only raised one-third
of it really. She has never been in the begging business before,
you see, and unfortunately I have had a good deal of experience in it."[13] This comment explains much of the situation. Since
the beginnings of BNSG, Homans had adequate or even generous financial support. While she did not spend funds lavishly
or unnecessarily, she had always had sufficient funds available
to her. The BNSG trustees rarely denied her requests, and she
had never had to solicit funds for the school.

Wellesley's decision to accept BNSG came on June 12, 1908,
when the Wellesley College Board of Trustees voted to accept
from the Boston Normal School of Gymnastics Trustees the sum
of $100,000.00 for continuing the programs of the Boston
Normal School of Gymnastics. The Wellesley trustees further
voted "That the President and Dean associate with themselves
three members of the Academic Council to determine such ac-

ademic adjustments as may be necessary in incorporating the Boston Normal School of Gymnastics as part of the College."[14]

By October the gifts and pledges for the new gymnasium reached $100,000.00 and J. A. Schweinfurth, the architect, was requested to submit plans for a gymnasium. The November report of the Wellesley College Gymnasium Committee credited the BNSG alumnae with raising $30,000.00, the Hemenway family with pledging half of the remainder, and "friends of the College" with the difference. A secret document, dated March 30, 1908, discloses that the "friends of the College" was President Caroline Hazard of Wellesley, who personally guaranteed $32,500.00 to complete the building fund for the gymnasium.[15]

With the documents of affiliation signed and the funds for a gymnasium in hand or pledged, Homans and Hazard turned to other problems of affiliation. The most pressing issues concerned the admission of students to the professional program in hygiene and physical education, the status of the professional students, and faculty appointments. In the first years of the merger students entered the hygiene and physical training course in one of three ways. First, candidates for the Wellesley B.A. could enroll in the program; second, students holding the bachelor's degree from other institutions could be admitted; and third, students could enter the two-year program much as they had at BNSG, except that they now had to meet, either by examination or certification, the requirements for admission to Wellesley.

The two-year students, who comprised the largest group for the first Wellesley years, had to have satisfied 15 "points" for admission. Each point represented the number of years ordinarily required to study each subject: "English—three points; History—one point; Mathematics—three points; Latin—four points; A Second Language (Greek or French or German [maximum])—three points; A Third Language (Greek or French or German[minimum]) or A Science: Chemistry or Physics—one point." Candidates had to be at least sixteen years of age, of good moral character and health and, for the hygiene and physical education program, free from organic disease and serious functional disorder, and possessing a keen sense of rhythm.[16]

Homans undoubtedly was delighted with the admission requirements which were beyond those of most physical training schools of the period.

Wellesley College fees were slightly higher than those of BNSG: $175.00 for tuition rather than $150.00 and $275.00 for room and board, comparable to that charged by the rooming houses in Boston. Wellesley classified the hygiene and physical education students as "special" and, as was true for Wellesley freshmen, they could not be accommodated in campus dormitories. Under the supervision of the college, the professional students lived in private homes in Wellesley village, about a mile from the new Wellesley gymnasium.

Homans announced the BNSG affiliation with Wellesley and the new admissions procedures in the 1908–1909 catalogue. "In September, 1909, the Boston Normal School of Gymnastics will become the Department of Hygiene and Physical Education of Wellesley College, Wellesley, Mass." [17] The announcement informed applicants that students in the professional hygiene and physical education course would enroll as special students. The BNSG catalogue also carried the Wellesley College calendar for 1909–1910 and a description of the new building erected especially to meet the demands of the professional program:

The construction of this building is in accordance with two specific purposes: first, to develop and extend the work of this School in the teaching of the art of health throughout the country, and in establishing the theoretical groundwork for such teaching; secondly, to provide for the students of Wellesley College the facilities necessary for a sound and systematic régime of physical training. [18]

The announcement clearly set forth Homans' priorities. The program to prepare teachers of hygiene and physical education remained her central focus. Although Homans valued Wellesley College and its standards of excellence, and she expected to offer Wellesley students a superior program in hygiene and physical education, of greater importance to her was the professional program to prepare women leaders in physical education. From the beginning of the merger her intent was clear—to create a rigorous undergraduate program in the liberal arts and sciences as a sound basis for an advanced or graduate program in physical education.

The rank and salary for BNSG faculty moving from a two-year private normal school to a four-year liberal arts faculty posed another problem. In BNSG's twenty years of existence Homans had always sought highly qualified faculty and appointed M.D.s and Ph.D.s when possible. The use of Harvard and MIT faculty to teach science and psychology courses helped Homans offer her students courses taught by outstanding faculty members. In addition, Homans employed local specialists on a part-time basis. Also, from the early years Homans had selected some especially well-qualified graduates to remain as assistants and, when she believed they were ready, she appointed them to the faculty. There was no need for academic ranks. Homans listed herself as director and the other faculty members as instructors, lecturers, and assistants.

At Wellesley, faculty members held academic ranks from instructor through professor, depending on their education and experience. When Durant founded Wellesley College in 1875 he appointed a woman president and sought qualified women for the faculty. Although at that time few women had the opportunity to acquire academic degrees, Durant found seven women professors and eleven other women whom he called teachers. Only one man, professor of music Charles H. Morse, was appointed to the first faculty. In the more than 30 years of Wellesley's existence, standards for academic preparation had risen and, by 1909, faculty members ranged from instructor to professor, a few more men had been appointed, and many faculty members held the Ph.D. degree. The large majority of the faculty were women who lived in small suites or rooms set aside for them in the dormitories. Wellesley salaries undoubtedly took this living arrangement into consideration. Homans looked with favor on the many women administrators and faculty members at Wellesley, who could be models for her students preparing to be heads of departments and directors of programs on college campuses.

BNSG's move to Wellesley coincided with the final year for two members of Wellesley's health and physical education faculty, Evelyn Barrett Sherrard and Lucille Eaton Hill. In 1906 the Wellesley trustees had reviewed the existing departments and combined the work in hygiene and physical education into one department, the Department of Hygiene and Physical Training, with Sherrard as department head. At that time both Sherrard and Hill received final three-year appointments.[19] The creation of a combined department suggests that the president and the trustees had discussed the direction of the work of both the health officer and the physical training faculty well before the BNSG affiliation and had decided to make the health of the students the basic rationale for a joint program.

Hill seemed bewildered by the changes and hurt by Wellesley's acceptance of Homans and BNSG. Affectionately known to the students as "Gym" Hill, she had joined the Wellesley faculty in the early 1880s. She had studied with Sargent but did not hold a bachelor's degree. Hill not only introduced the Sargent system of gymnastics to Wellesley, but also encouraged sport and dance, planned and produced festivals, and was active in physical education professional associations. She even engaged in some research to demonstrate that sport activities such as crew produced physiological results comparable to gymnastics. A member of the class of 1907 wrote "Miss Hill gave to Wellesley two of its loveliest pageants—Float Night and Tree Day. These were evolved through her interest in organized sports and natural dancing. . . . Her enthusiasm and zest for life were boundless, and she had a genius for imparting enthusiasm to her students."[20] Ruth C. Hanford recalled "her work has meant so much to us, not only in physical education, but in the real appreciation of all things beautiful."[21]

When Homans' plans became known, Hill poured out her feelings in a letter to Hitchcock at Amherst College:

My beloved "system" is sold out as you know! It is a heartbreaking thing to have one's child without his clothes on! But I want you to know I believe in and try to practice "Spiritual Athletics" and I have faith that in some way, in the end, the splendid ideals the students so sincerely are working for will be recognized by the "Powers that Be."[22]

Hill and Homans held opposite views concerning the purpose of gymnastics and physical activities. Hill valued joy as well as physical vigor, and instilled a love of sport and dance in her students. While Homans did not object to students enjoying physical activities, she stressed the responsibility of each student to attain physical vigor and robust health through physical activities. She encouraged "forms of exercise as may be done alone. . . . The student, like the average person, is too dependent upon the company of others, in the matter of exercise as well as in other respects."[23] In spite of philosophical differences between the two women, Homans provided the undergraduates with more indoor and outdoor facilities, more faculty, and more curricular and recreational offerings than had Hill.

As Homans began incorporating her ideas and philosophy at Wellesley, she appointed well-qualified faculty members to serve both the professional and undergraduate students. The move to Wellesley severed BNSG's connections with Harvard and MIT. Now that the Wellesley College faculty members were available to teach the professional students, Josiah Royce of Harvard University, Elliott G. Brackett of Harvard Medical School, Louis Derr and Fred L. Bardwell of MIT, Gilbert of the Gilbert School of Social Dancing, Jean Gelás in fencing, and Christian Eberhard, the director of the Boston Athletic Association, would no longer teach Homans' students. In addition, Sarah A. Bond, medical examiner and lecturer in symptomatology and emergencies, Edward Blake Barton, instructor in the theory and practice of teaching, Wilhelmina C. Molock, instructor in anthropometry and games, Sarah Davis '07, assistant and instructor in corrective gymnastics, and the pianist, Margaret Johnson '03, did not make the move to Wellesley.

Two Wellesley staff members remained on the staff in 1909–1910—the resident physician, Katherine Piatt Raymond, B.S., M.D., and a BNSG alumna, Estella May Fearon '06, B.S. Four members of the BNSG faculty and staff assumed teaching positions at Wellesley—Carl Oscar Louis Collin, M.D.; Frederick H. Pratt, M.A., M.D.; Loretto Fish Carney '93 and Annie Chapin Stedman '95. New appointments for 1909–1910 included instructors Eunice Blanche Sterling '00, M.D., Edna Lois Williams '07, and Marion Wheeler Hartwell '07; and an assistant medical examiner, Sophie Goudge Laws, M.D.[24] The salaries of

Collin, Pratt, Carney, and Stedman, the faculty members who moved from BNSG to Wellesley as instructors, were not announced, but Ellen Fitz Pendleton, acting Wellesley president, disclosed that "the scale of salaries at the Normal School was evidently in excess of those of the College."[25]

Homans, 60 years of age with nineteen years of experience as director of BNSG, no bachelor's degree, and an honorary M.A., presented the greatest problem of rank and salary. Pendleton wrote Hazard, who was on leave for health reasons:

The other matter which I find it difficult to decide is . . . the question of the new department of Hygiene and Physical Training. The Committee left the question of Miss Homan's [sic] title and salary to me with power to adjust. . . . I wrote you I think in my last letter what her present salary is ($3500). I have seen her in regard to it and I think that it will be a disappointment to her if the same salary is not continued. I think she is willing to accept the title of *Director* of the Department of Hygiene and Physical Training, though I think she would be glad if some other title could be thought of. She herself sees the inappropriateness of the title of *professor*, and does not wish it, and I presume that we shall settle on the title of Director. She is eager to have the name of the department changed from Hygiene and Physical Training to Physical Education and Hygiene. I am very much inclined to recommend the change from Physical Training to Physical Education, but I am inclined also to keep the order as it is at present.[26]

In late March Pendleton appointed Homans director of the Department of Hygiene and Physical Education at $3,500.00 for the first year and $2,500.00 for the following two years. At $3,500.00 Homans became one of the highest paid faculty members at Wellesley. She partly had her way in the name of the department but did not have her way in the matter of salary. In Wellesley's yearly *Bulletin* the officers of instruction were listed according to rank in the order of appointment. In the 1909–1910 *Bulletin* 21 professors precede Homans, many of them distinguished scholars such as Charlotte Fitch Roberts in chemistry and Katharine Lee Bates in English literature. Below the professors and above the associate professors is Amy Morris Homans, M.A., listed as director of the Department of Hygiene and Physical Education.

In all probability Homans had investigated the salaries at Wellesley and was prepared for the lower salary. Wellesley may or may not have known that Homans' income benefited from the Hemenway estate. With BNSG's affiliation with Wellesley, Homans and her sister Gertrude gave up the house provided for them by Hemenway at 26 Berwick Park and moved to Wellesley. The BNSG trustees arranged an annuity of $800 which approximated the benefits the sisters received from living in the Berwick Park house. The annuity was paid half to Homans and half to her sister Gertrude during their lives, and the whole sum to the survivor during her life.[27] Thus, the ties with Boston, where Homans had lived during many professionally rewarding years, were severed.

During this period Homans began to receive professional recognition for her accomplishments. Her biography appeared in the 1908–1909 edition of *Who's Who in America* and, in the spring of 1908, Bates College near her home in Maine had conferred on her an Honorary Master's degree.[28] At age 60, Homans had fulfilled another dream—the attainment of a college degree. When she joined the faculty of Wellesley, she did so with an academic degree, even if it had not been earned in the classroom.

9

Homans at Wellesley: Liberal Arts and Professional Education

For Homans, the Wellesley years began when the Wellesley College Board of Trustees voted to accept the sum of $100,000.00 from the trustees under the will of Mary Hemenway for the purpose of training teachers of gymnastics. Hazard, who so badly wanted a gymnasium for the college, suffered ill health and submitted her resignation in September, 1908, but was persuaded, instead, to take a year's leave of absence. Thus many of the final arrangements for the merger of BNSG with Wellesley were made by acting President Ellen Fitz Pendleton. Fund raising, supervising the building, furnishing the gymnasium, and making the necessary academic adjustments proceeded simultaneously.

In June, 1908, the Wellesley Trustees appointed a committee to proceed with building the gymnasium before the winter of 1909, if possible. The committee—George Howe Davenport, Cornelia Warren, and Alpheus Holmes Hardy, the treasurer of the Board of Trustees—recommended that the gymnasium be placed near the present athletic grounds on the plateau west of Cazenove dormitory in a far corner of the campus.[1] With Schweinfurth appointed as architect, the planning began. Having directed BNSG for almost twenty years, knowing the courses taught in the curriculum and the clinic work at the Children's Hospital, visiting other professional training schools, and viewing the future needs of professional physical education programs, Homans specified exactly what she wanted: appropriate administrative offices; rooms for medical examinations; gymnasiums for gymnastics, dancing, and indoor games; laboratories, lecture rooms, and a library; dressing and bathing facilities; offices for faculty members; and proper storage for everything from gymnasium suits to laboratory equipment. In January, 1909, Schweinfurth submitted plans for a gymnasium containing everything Homans demanded, at a cost of $135,000.00—$30,000.00 more than the amount of money which had been raised or pledged. Both Homans and Pendleton felt strongly that nothing could be omitted from the building. Homans wanted the best possible building as a showcase for professional programs and Pendleton realized that a smaller building might provide less space for the undergraduate students. To her, one of the most attractive features of the proposed new building was *two* gymnasiums, one large and one small, so that two classes could be conducted at the same time.

Homans' continuing efforts to raise funds brought only $16,000.00 of the necessary $30,000.00. Recognizing the gravity of the situation, Schweinfurth, Pendleton, and Homans conferred and, finally, decided that there would be two plans. At the time the construction started, the available money would determine which plan would be used.[2] At one time there had been a suggestion to postpone the building and occupy temporary quarters, but that idea was no longer considered. The fateful decision came in March when, with less than the $135,000.00 for the gymnasium, construction began on the smaller building.

The new three-story structure, named Mary Hemenway Hall, included a large, well-lighted, high-ceilinged gymnasium at right angles to the rear of the main building. The street floor of the main building housed the administrative offices, the medical examining rooms, and laboratories for anthropometry and corrective gymnastics; the second floor contained a large library and study as well as two lecture rooms; and on the third floor were the laboratories for anatomy, physiology, and hygiene. Attractive faculty offices were placed on each floor. The large gymnasium was equipped with the latest Swedish gymnastics equipment. The floor below the gymnasium was a marvel of the 1910s:

Here will be a complete system of baths . . . designed with reference to safety, speed, and efficiency. The partitioned baths will be under a unique form of central control, whereby individual as well as general requirements will be met by means of an operator stationed at the supply levers.[3]

Mary Hemenway Hall, Wellesley College gymnasium, c. 1910

The shower room contained 60 individual marble shower rooms with a large dressing room on either side, each with 60 individual dressing rooms. After each activity class, students removed their gymnasium costumes and, covering themselves with a large white sheet, proceeded to individual shower stalls. A matron stationed in the glassed-in control room regulated the showers, turning on water of approved temperatures for a specified period of time. Although such regimentation is difficult to imagine today, this latest hygienic development was a wonder of the times.

Homans approved the new gymnasium on November 15, 1909, on her 61st birthday. In a rare instance of sharing her feelings, she sent a hand-written note to Hazard:

As you doubtless know, I met Mr. Davenport at Mary Hemenway Hall this afternoon to approve the building for his acceptance for the College—For me it has been the great event of my 61st birthday. I am never unmindful that except for you, the great possibilities for service now open to me, would have been lost—I am glad every day to owe this to you—Will you share my birthday flowers with me[?][4]

Finally, the new gymnasium, not yet complete in every detail, opened as planned for the fall semester, 1909. Accepted from the architect in November, the building was dedicated on December 7, 1909:

Wellesley's new gymnasium, named Mary Hemenway Hall, in memory of the founder of the Boston Normal School of Gymnastics, now the Wellesley College department of hygiene and physical education, was formally opened this afternoon with exercises beginning at half-past two o'clock, under the charge of President Hazard and Miss Amy M. Homans, director of this new gymnasium and of the newly reorganized department. Officers of the college and practically all of the members of the faculty, many alumnae and friends of the college were in attendance upon these exercises and shared in the general enthusiasm over Wellesley's acquisition of this commodious, thoroughly equipped and much needed building.[5]

Recasting BNSG's curriculum required many meetings and discussions for well over six months. Characteristically, Homans did not delegate that responsibility to anyone else, but made all the arrangements herself. At times, she seemed to move slowly on curricular matters. Pendleton reported to Hazard on December 23, 1908:

I have had one or two talks with Miss Homans, but as yet the committee of the Faculty has not met her. This Committee consists of Miss Whiting, Miss Roberts, Miss Willcox, Miss Calkins, Miss McKeag, and Dr. Raymond. I have tried to put on everybody who would be especially interested in the work of the students who could come to us from the school. Miss Homans preferred not to have the committee meet until after the Christmas holidays.[6]

The committee members represented academic departments in which the new students might take courses. Raymond was the resident physician; Whiting taught physics; Roberts, chemistry; and Calkins, philosophy and physiology. The BNSG curriculum included courses in each area, some of which had been taught by BNSG faculty at BNSG, others by Harvard professors at BNSG, and still others by MIT professors at MIT, and would now be conducted by the Wellesley faculty.

In arranging for these courses at Wellesley, a controversy arose over teaching the physiology course. Willcox believed the zoology and physiology department should teach the course, and Homans preferred to have it taught in the new laboratories in the gymnasium. Finally, Pendleton asked Willcox to name an outside authority whose opinion she would respect. She suggested Professor Sedgwick from MIT. Nothing could have been more fortunate for Homans. In the early days Sedgwick taught biology to the BNSG students and knew Hemenway, Homans, and the BNSG program. Sedgwick proposed that the physiology for the hygiene and physical education students be given in the hygiene department and that basic physiology be offered in the zoology and physiology department. He also assured Pendleton that it would be difficult to obtain a faculty member who was prepared in both pure physiology and applied physiology, such as that required for the professional students.[7] Of course, the decision pleased Homans, and Pendleton proceeded according to the suggestions made by Sedgwick.

At Wellesley the first-year students enrolled in college classes in anatomy, chemistry, physics, and English composition in special sections open only to students enrolled in the hygiene and physical education professional program. This plan was necessary because the course work differed considerably from the undergraduate studies at Wellesley. For example, elementary chemistry and physics were two-semester courses for Wellesley undergraduates, but one-semester courses for the professional students. Anatomy, another required subject in the professional curriculum, was added to the offerings of the zoology and physiology department. Homans must have been pleased to add English composition to the curriculum even though it met for only one hour a week. Homans could now reassure herself that her students had the benefits of composition taught in a strong liberal arts college.

Departmental courses for the first-year students included kinesiology, Swedish gymnastics, corrective gymnastics and emergencies, and classes in gymnastic games, dancing, swimming, and athletics. Wellesley's excellent outdoor fields adjacent to the gymnasium made a strong athletic and sports program possible.

The senior or second-year program at Wellesley followed the BNSG curriculum with minor changes. Basic physiology was taught in the zoology department and applied physiology in the hygiene and physical education department. The students enrolled in education and psychology courses offered in the education department. The rest of the program was departmental and focused on advanced gymnastics and on the theory and art of teaching. Sterling, who conducted the college health clinic, supervised second-year students in giving corrective gymnastics and taught symptomatology. History of physical education and anthropometry completed the theoretical courses in the second year. The students also practiced athletics and outdoor games in the spring and fall. Added to this full program, the second-year students taught either in the local public schools or in college classes, but always under supervision.

Mindful of the charge to provide Wellesley students with a strong program aimed at improving and maintaining their health, the new department continued to give medical examinations to entering students. Raymond taught a one-hour required course in hygiene which focused on the structure and function of the body and the general principles of personal and public health. Students whose medical examination revealed a condition which could be improved by exercise were required to enroll in corrective gymnastics. Other students could select courses from a variety of activities such as archery, basketball, golf, field hockey, rowing, running, or tennis in the fall and spring. Fencing, riding, and swimming were available for an

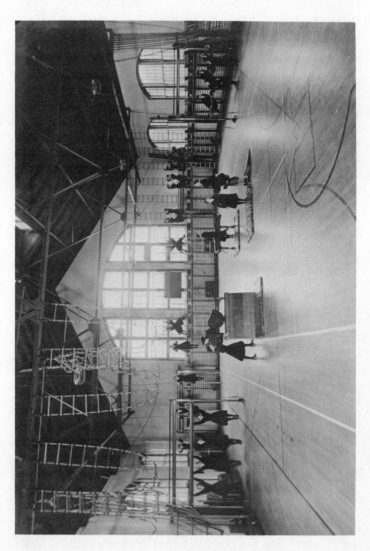

Gymnastics, Wellesley College gymnasium, c. 1910

additional fee. The indoor activities added a third level of gymnastics and dancing, separated into one course for freshman and seniors and one for sophomores and juniors. A new indoor course on games, plays, and folk dancing was designed for students who planned to work in settlement houses, playgrounds, or elementary schools.

Not only did the department have the responsibility for the instructional program in hygiene and physical education activities, but it also supervised the college recreational program, including the Athletic Association, sport clubs, and special events. Typical of the period and in keeping with Hill's philosophy, Homans and her faculty controlled the recreational offerings, permitting only inter-class competition. Intercollegiate meets were frowned on as unnecessary and possibly as copying the men's programs already severely criticized for semiprofessionalism. With the overriding need to stress femininity in women's sports, Homans conducted a broad recreational and intramural program for the Wellesley students. The Athletic Association, in existence since 1896, sponsored two important field days each year. Homans took her responsibilities with the Athletic Association as seriously as she did her academic duties. She attended the Fall Field Day her first year and watched the four classes compete for the athletic honors.[8]

The public enjoyed two occasions which showcased departmental events, the Tree Day dance pageant and Float Night. Tree Day, initiated by students in the second year of the college and encouraged by Durant to increase the number of trees on the large campus, began as a simple tree-planting ceremony. Over the years costumes, orations, a march of the classes were added, and, in 1889, a pageant with dances. Hill, credited with introducing "picture dancing," used it widely in Tree Day pageants and left a legacy which was treasured by students and alumnae. Float Night, earlier called "Float," grew from a simple sunset gathering of boats on Lake Waban followed by singing and the lighting of lanterns to guide the boats to shore. By the 1890s Wellesley's "Float Day" had become a major attraction in the Boston area with special trains from Boston to Wellesley.[9] Wisely, Homans continued both traditions. Having settled such undergraduate matters, Homans turned her attention to the lives of the professional students at Wellesley.

Tree Day dancing, Wellesley College, c. 1906

In the first year of the merger, 64 professional students enrolled in the department—51 from BNSG and thirteen new students. Five Wellesley students entered the five-year program leading first to a Wellesley B.S., and then to a Wellesley College Certificate in Hygiene and Physical Education at the end of the fifth year. Along with some 300 other Wellesley freshmen, the hygiene and physical education students lived in the village of Wellesley; however, they were easily identified. Homans made no distinction between Boston's city streets and the Wellesley campus, and while other students strode around the campus in their shirtwaists, casual skirts and other fashions of the day, the new special students walked primly through the village and campus to the new gymnasium wearing hats and gloves, while also carrying books and sport equipment. Charlotte Rey Burr '09–'10 dedicated a song to this custom:

> Oh we wear hats on our cocoons
> And no rats or rolls;
> Dickies in our gym fronts,
> And all such things as those.[10]

> We all wear holeproof stockings,
> And orthopedic shoes,
> And we never go out walking
> With our beaux—ah me.[11]

The tune began:

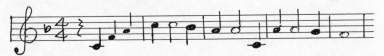

Classes began at 9 o'clock a.m. and lasted until 4:00 o'clock p.m. or later with a crowded schedule of lectures, gymnastics, sports, dance, laboratories, and study. Most classes were conducted in Mary Hemenway Hall and even the English composition instructor came to the gymnasium to teach her class. The professional students dashed to College Hall for physics, zoology, and other Wellesley courses and to the chemistry building for chemistry. Chemistry class followed lunch and proved to be a difficult time for some students to stay awake. The sympathetic chemistry professor is reported to have said to one student about to wake up her neighbor, "Let her sleep. She's tired."[12]

Just as she had at BNSG, Homans monitored the students' behavior in and out of the classroom. Morning assemblies were not possible, but Homans often entered a classroom and talked with the students just before the class began. In these brief remarks Homans set the standards for Wellesley women in physical education. She believed firmly that a high sense of vocation and the capacity to endure hard work were essential for success. These qualities were those subtly inculcated in young men

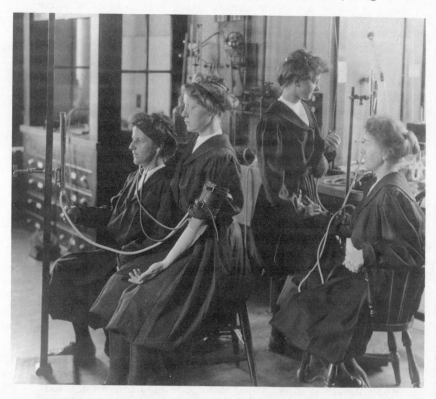

Physiology laboratory, Mary Hemenway Hall, Wellesley College, c. 1913

as they moved into adulthood but, ordinarily, were not considered part of a young woman's education. Homans, mindful of the importance of such characteristics, constantly stressed the need for ability, endurance, and conquering personal weakness.

Mabel Lee, the frail underweight student who had been threatened with expulsion in the fall of 1909 unless she gained weight, recounts an example of conquering personal weakness.

Among the new Swedish equipment in the gymnasium at Wellesley were climbing ropes which hung like a giant portiere from a crossbeam near the 45-foot ceiling. A gymnastic feat which the students learned was climbing diagonally from one rope to the next while ascending and descending. The gymnast moved from the floor on one side of the room, grasping each rope higher and higher until she reached the ceiling and the last rope simultaneously. The gymnast then descended the ropes in reverse order, moving lower on each rope, until she returned to the starting point. Day by day the seniors began climbing the ropes, moving across to reach the high crossbeam on the other side of the gymnasium and descending in the same fashion. One day Collin "broke into an impish grin" and pointed his finger at Lee, asking her to perform the entire routine.

Lee began her ordeal with Collin moving below, encouraging her, while her classmates waited breathlessly. After she reached the last rope at the top of the other side of the gymnasium, she rested a moment before beginning her return. At Collin's bidding a student slipped out of the room and returned followed by Homans. Slowly and carefully, as if proving herself not only to Collin but also to Homans, Lee arrived successfully back at the first rope as she touched the floor. Lee recalls that she "crumpled in a heap to the floor." Helping her up, Collin turned to Homans and triumphantly said, "I told you she could do it." The only sound as Homans walked slowly out of the gymnasium was the rustle of her petticoats.[13]

Gifts for the new building continued to arrive and made special purchases possible. In May, 1910, Hazard reported that Mrs. Mary C. Scott presented $5,000.00, in memory of her mother, to the Department of Hygiene and Physical Education for the library of the new building. The Edith Hemenway Eustis Memorial Fund was divided into two amounts, $3,000.00 for immediate use and $2,000.00 for investment, the income of which was to be used to purchase books.[14]

Homans, BNSG faculty, and the professional students adapted quickly to life at Wellesley. Homans had especially enjoyed and been professionally stimulated by her contacts with Hazard whom she respected and with whom she worked closely for over two years. In contrast to the joyous note to Hazard on the occasion

of accepting the completed gymnasium, she now revealed her
sense of loss when Hazard resigned in 1910:

I dare not think of its [Hazard's resignation] effect upon my department—for fifteen years I have worked absolutely alone—your cooperation has made all things possible—it has vitalized everything. Because of it, the work must succeed. I do not know how.[15]

Rarely did Homans express her personal feelings. The fifteen
years she referred to represented the period since Hemenway's
death. After her death there was never a hint of loneliness or
a need of others' support. The note to Hazard offers an unusual glimpse of Homans as a person who valued the support
and encouragement of others.

Hazard presented her final report as president of Wellesley
College in 1910. In it she expressed her support of the new hygiene and physical education program:

One of the prime objects of the College . . . is the training of Christian teachers. With this new department, under the guidance of Miss
Homans, Wellesley is fulfilling this task in a new direction. . . . The
department of Hygiene and Physical Education at Wellesley is a new
departure for a college, for it definitely undertakes not only to instruct
college students in ways of right living, but to train such as elect special
courses in the department to teach hygiene in other places. It seems
to me a very important development of the College. Without health a
woman's life is sadly handicapped. She is the natural guardian of the
health of children. To maintain and improve her own health, whatever her walk in life, is one of the prime essentials of living; to instill
right principles in those under her care is one of her highest duties.
The department definitely undertakes to prepare her for these duties,
and I beg that the Trustees will follow this work, now in its beginning
with fostering care.[16]

Hazard, who had first listened to Homans' proposal to merge
BNSG with Wellesley and initiate an innovative program for
professional women, had made it possible to complete the gymnasium. She recognized Homans' strong leadership and further realized the extent of financial support to which she had
been accustomed. Hazard hoped Homans could adapt to the
demands of a college community with committees, deans, and

administrative officers who expected strict adherence to academic regulation, budgets, and trustee decisions. Hazard's final report, begging the trustees to foster the program, gave Homans encouragement.

The first year of the merger had gone well. The Academic Council had supported Homans' request for academic credit for hygiene and physical education, and the Wellesley academic departments had been able to adapt the course work to meet the needs of the new department. The problem of who would teach physiology had proved difficult, but it had been solved. Further, Homans had agreed to a decrease in her salary to bring it more in line with other professors. Many members of the Wellesley College faculty gradually began to understand Homans' goals and that she was not a typical gym teacher. They realized that she intended to direct a "Department which stood for the very highest ideals in general education not admitting for a moment that physical education . . . could be carried on apart from intellectual and ethical training."[17] Now Homans turned her attention to her cherished dream of a graduate program for women in physical education.

10

The Wellesley Image in Physical Education for Women

In the few years remaining before her retirement in 1918, Homans renewed her efforts to create a profession of physical education for women. Still vigorous and professionally active, she wrote to Augustus Hemenway that she would "like a long holiday, but there are certain things that I must accomplish for the Department before I leave it. It must be adequate for all future needs and my plans are made to that end."[1] While she did not neglect the programs for the Wellesley undergraduates, her primary interest lay in achieving graduate status for the professional program at Wellesley and maintaining her high standards for the professional and personal behavior of her students.

Wellesley offered Homans a strong base for achieving her goals. Rather than functioning as a private two-year normal school occupying rooms in a Boston building, at Wellesley Homans operated from within a strong institution which pioneered women's higher education. She had a well-planned, thoroughly modern gymnasium, unusually fine outdoor facilities, programs for undergraduate students, and a program for professional hygiene and physical education students which she hoped would soon be a graduate program. She did not dismiss the undergraduate programs lightly and strengthened that curriculum as she worked toward a graduate program for the professional students.

After Wellesley's undergraduate curriculum prescribed courses in hygiene and physical education for the degree, all undergraduate students were required to enroll in a hygiene course. The course focused on basic physiology, hygienic practices, posture, and the place of physical education in a liberal arts education. Eugene Howe taught the course for years, beginning in 1914, earning himself the nickname, "Eugene Hygiene." In a letter written shortly after he started teaching the course and showing some concern over a man teaching hygiene to women students, Howe wrote:

So far I am fairly satisfied. I find I can swing a lecture fairly untrammeled by notes, make them laugh, and quiet them down at will, as a rule. They apparently . . . are without timidity at a man's teaching the subject, and have no intention of baiting a "solemn *young* man." For one thing I have not been solemn.[2]

In addition to the hygiene course, the undergraduate students took an activity course in the freshmen and sophomore years. By Homans' final year at Wellesley the department offered instruction in archery, baseball, basketball, golf, field hockey, horseback riding, rowing, running, and tennis. However, clinging to its gymnastics heritage, the winter work continued to offer Swedish gymnastics. The seniors, or second-year professional students, assisted in the sport and gymnastics instruction. At times, the Wellesley freshmen and sophomores objected to the professional students as teachers, some of them no older than the sophomores, and, according to the undergraduates, unnecessarily strict. The professional students, on the other hand, probably were frightened of teaching students their own age and made mistakes as they learned to cope with classes.

Student recreation was an important part of Homans' plans for a complete physical education program, and she made every effort to provide excellent facilities for the Wellesley students. When she arrived, the college had six tennis courts, one hockey field, and two basketball fields in addition to the Nehoiden Golf Club operated by the college in cooperation with the town of Wellesley. By 1913 Wellesley could boast of fourteen tennis courts, four basketball courts, two hockey fields, and an archery range. Homans continued to advise the Athletic Association and in her last year at Wellesley presented a Riding Cup for competition in horseback riding. In the fall of 1917 Homans addressed the Athletic Association about her hope for a swimming pool and later that fall entertained the student leaders at dinner at the Wellesley Inn.

While Homans conscientiously developed an excellent undergraduate hygiene and physical education program, she concentrated most of her attention on attaining graduate status for the professional program and furthering the advancement of physical education for women. Homans made her intentions clear in the 1911–1912 *Bulletin*. "Ultimately admission to this course will be limited to applicants who are candidates for the B.A. degree at Wellesley College and to those who already hold the Bachelor's degree either from Wellesley or from some other college."[3] At that time graduate work in physical education was offered at Columbia University, Oberlin College, Springfield College, and the Normal College of the American Gymnastic Union.[4] While three of these programs were available to women, only one was in the East and none was exclusively for women. Homans, aware of the need for women leaders and the education for leadership which she could provide, planned to offer a model graduate course in hygiene and physical education for women.

Homans made the necessary changes in the faculty to obtain highly qualified professors for graduate level work. In 1915 Homans received the title of Professor of Hygiene and Physical Education, fulfilling a life-long dream. The 1909 department faculty of one director, seven instructors, and one assistant increased in six years to one director and professor, two associate professors, one assistant professor, six instructors, two assistants, a recorder, a librarian, and a curator. In 1912 William Skarstrom '95, M.D., began his long association with Wellesley as an associate professor and, in 1914, Eugene Howe, Ph.D., who had joined the faculty as an instructor, was promoted to associate professor. Homans continued to appoint outstanding BNSG alumnae as Wellesley faculty, sometimes preparing them to move to important positions in other institutions. From 1909 to 1918 Edna Manship '01, Gertrude Manchester '13, Sarah Davis '07, and Elizabeth Halsey '16 taught at Wellesley and later accepted appointments at well–known colleges and universities.

1918 Field Day, Wellesley College

Expectations of faculty included the traditional academic functions of teaching, research, and service. Homans knew that excellent qualifications would be necessary to have a graduate program approved and that the continued placement of Wellesley students in good positions depended on an outstanding faculty. In 1915–1916 Howe published articles in the *American Journal of Public Health* and the *Physical Education Review*. One faculty member, Fette, taught at the summer session at Columbia University and Skarstrom served on the summer faculty of the National Board of the YWCA in New York and Los Angeles. Also, Manship studied dancing that year. Typical of college teachers of any period, Davis complained that there was not enough time for research, which prevented many interesting problems from being investigated.[5] Homans and Skarstrom served on Wellesley's Academic Council committees, Homans on the Student Entertainment Committee and later the Graduate Council, and Skarstrom on the Constitution Committee.

In 1913 Homans successfully maneuvered a name-change of the department to the Department of Hygiene. The omission of "physical education" represents her search for an encompassing term for the many sciences and physical activities which she believed necessary for an optimal program. *Hygiene* could be interpreted to mean a science basic to the establishment and maintenance of health rather than the present-day meaning of conditions and practices conducive to health. Always rigorous, courses had originally been planned for the typical undergraduate student of the 1890s and to the applied needs of professional students. Now, in preparation for a graduate program, the faculty gradually strengthened their courses toward graduate level.

Establishing a graduate program in physical education created special problems. Wellesley conferred the Master of Arts degree, requiring fifteen hours of college work, a thesis or report based on independent work, and a reading knowledge of French or German. One year of residency was required, "but two or more years are usually needed for the completion of the work."[6] Such a program was not planned to prepare students for a professional career. The faculty sought a somewhat different approach and an appropriate degree or title "which will sound bigger than 'certificate,' which will not be an anticlimax after the A.B., and which will not imply too great superiority of the A.B."[7] A serious proposal was made to consider a B.S. in Hygiene which would be granted after five years at Wellesley with a master's degree in two additional years. Finally, the department retained the title "Certificate."

By 1915 a definite time table had been set to change the professional program to a graduate program. The 1915 *Bulletin* announced, "After the academic year 1916–1917 admission to this course will be limited to applicants who are candidates for the B.A. degree at Wellesley College and to those who already hold the Bachelor's degree from Wellesley College or from some other college."[8] As the time approached, more and more entering students held the bachelor's degree. The last class which Homans admitted was the first class at the graduate level. The students had been graduated from a variety of colleges and universities including Bates, Sweet Briar, Mount Holyoke, Smith, Wellesley, Radcliffe, Pomona, North Carolina State Normal, Grinnell, Vassar, and Rockford. Other students came from the Universities of Wisconsin, Washington, Chicago, California, and Minnesota, Leland Stanford University, and Iowa State University.[9]

Several years after Homans' retirement, Wellesley offered both the Certificate and the M.A. based on Wellesley's degree requirements. The Committee on Graduate Instruction approved the plan for a master's degree submitted by Josephine Rathbone Karpovich '22. In 1923, Wellesley awarded the first master's degrees in hygiene to Karpovich, Vivian Collins '22, Elizabeth Halsey '16, and Carol Rice '22. In 1926 the Master of Arts was changed to a Master of Science in Hygiene and Physical Education.

These older, more mature students underwent the same careful scrutiny by Homans as had the younger students. Some of them smarted under Homans' admonitions, while others, more tolerant, recognized Homans as a revered leader in physical education and understood the reasons for her attention to such matters. Even in her last years at Wellesley, Homans maintained her practice of eliminating as quickly as possible personal "traits or habits which would militate against success."[10]

Class of 1919, First graduate class, Department of Hygiene and Physical Education, Wellesley College

Tales of angry tears and miserable hours recovering from a session with Homans exist. Many students considered her a tyrant. A summons to Miss Homans' office continued to bring fear, and sometimes terror, to the students. When Homans' secretary, whom the students secretly named the "Angel of Death," quietly appeared in the doorway of a classroom or gymnasium, every woman held her breath until she announced the name of the student who was to report *immediately* to Homans' office. The summoned student followed the secretary back to the office, straightening her hair, brushing her collar, and trying to remember what she had done during the last few days. A call from the "Angel of Death" could mean dismissal, a brief session to improve the student's posture or walk, a reminder to wear a hat in the village, or an inquiry about the student's health. Gladys Gorman '16 relates:

She always looked steadily at me, and always there was an incipient twinkle in her eyes. Every time, two things happened—she would question me about my meals—was I eating enough, and enough of the right things—did I get any rest during the day. That stumped me, for the schedule laid out for us by the Department left no time for even one extra long breath while on the run. She said that she and the other members of the staff were concerned about my "high color" or pink cheeks—ever since I could recall, physical activity on my part had resulted in pink cheeks, and I managed to muster enough courage to convey this phenomenon to her. It was the fact, however, that she knew I had roomed my junior year with a classmate who had TB (and a couple of years later died of it) made me realize that she did have information about every student in her department, and that she was interested in each one individually as a person.[11]

While there was no formal probation period at Wellesley, Homans dismissed students who had physical handicaps such as deafness or who she thought could not become successful physical educators. Just as in the BNSG days, it was not unusual for Homans to request an undergraduate professional student to remain an additional year to gain more experience or maturity.

Many students believed Homans had an uncanny knack of knowing their every act and, sometimes it seemed, their very thoughts. One incident involved an anatomy course in which the students dissected cats thoroughly preserved in formaldehyde.

When some of the students decided they should take their partially dissected cats to the dormitory to study, they carefully wrapped them in oilcloth and tied them to their bicycles. Safely ensconced in their third-floor rooms and busy memorizing bones, muscles, tendons, and ligaments, the students did not hear the approach of the Irish maid, Emmy, who became almost hysterical at the sight of the cats. Somehow, Homans learned of the incident and, as expected, reprimanded the students for removing laboratory materials and for creating a disturbance unbecoming to young ladies.[12]

As in the BNSG days, Homans expected students to know and obey her favorite lines from Shakespeare, "Her voice was ever soft, gentle and low; an excellent thing in woman." Most of them heeded the motto, at least in Mary Hemenway Hall, but late one afternoon when Homans was thought to be out of town, women of the class of '13, after their last activity class of the day, raised their voices loud and clear while dressing in their individual cubicles in the large dressing room. Led by Florence Lawson who had a trained soprano voice, they began an operatic rendition of the famous lines. They all joined in until the dressing rooms resounded with loud voices, interspersed with bursts of laughter. Wilma Haynes, whose dressing cubicle was nearest the door, suddenly realized that Homans had entered the room. She tried unsuccessfully to tap a signal to the cubicle next to her, but could not be heard. In a brief break in the singing, Homans said quietly, "Young ladies." Instantly, the singing stopped. The inevitable meeting followed with appropriate remarks about professional behavior and attitudes, but also with a twinkle in Homans' eyes showing that she understood the need to release their young, boisterous spirits.

On another occasion, Homans showed amusement and relief when she finally tracked down what she thought was an exclusive student club, the Wood Nymphs. With her strong belief in democracy, she discouraged organizations that might exclude some students. She eventually learned that her fears were groundless. The only qualifications for membership in the Wood Nymphs was the lack of talent in ballet or natural dancing. The Nymphs simply shared the misery and embarrassment of a required activity in which they did not perform well.[13]

As the social life of the period became less formal, Homans joined in some student activities. One story tells of a picnic, at which Homans was grateful to Skarstrom for finding her a rock on which she could perch rather than sitting on the ground with the students.[14] She ate her first ice cream cone or "hokey-po-key" at a party for the class of '14 held at the home of Ruth Elliott '14 in suburban Brighton.[15]

However, proper professional behavior was always Homans' first concern. Through her talks to groups of students, individual conferences, and social situations she conveyed the superiority of Wellesley's professional program in hygiene and their obligation to live up to Wellesley's and Homans' high ideals. Many students recall that she had a great deal to say about becoming a professional woman. Homans' prescription for success included an expertise in physical education, a clear vision of the goals of physical education, high standards, the ability to stand up under criticism, the willingness to work hard, and a zest for life.

College and university presidents sought Wellesley women to fill positions in physical education for women. Homans' knowledge of her students and their strengths and weaknesses made her a reliable source for good teachers and administrators. She made straightforward recommendations: "I send ——— to you with no question of her success. . . . You will be proud of [her] as a member of your faculty."[16] About another student she wrote, "That girl is going to make a name for herself," and of still another, "——— is a gentlewoman, a fine type, and she is a splendid all-around progressive teacher." Homans asked penetrating questions about her graduates: "I wish you would tell me definitely if ——— is strong in athletics."[17] Even as she approached 70 years of age, she had an uncanny ability to suggest just the right woman for a particular position. For the occasional student she asked to remain and teach at Wellesley, she made it clear that it was a learning experience. Halsey '16 told of an individual conference at which Homans criticized her severely, detailing her every fault, and then invited Halsey to teach at Wellesley.[18]

When Homans moved to Wellesley her careful placement of BNSG graduates had created a network of alumnae who had become a major influence in the development of physical education for women. During the next few years she extended her network to 28 states, Hawaii, Canada, China, and Japan. By 1916, 621 students had been graduated from BNSG and Wellesley's professional program in hygiene and physical education. One hundred twenty-six, or over one-third, held the title "director" and were in positions to help Homans shape the direction of women's physical education.[19] Of the 126, 39 directed departments in institutions of higher learning.[20] By this time the criteria of a profession of physical education for women were discernible. Homans stressed the humanitarian or service objectives of physical education and guided her students in defining a philosophy of physical education for women. She encouraged the development of knowledge in physical education and at the same time molded her alumnae and other women in physical education into a cohesive professional community.

11

The Professionalization of Physical Education for Women

"Professionalization" was an unknown term in 1910, but from an analysis of Homans' actions and from today's perspective, it well describes Homans' activities in women's physical education from 1910 to 1918. During her ten years at Wellesley, Homans undertook several strategies to strengthen the professional community of women physical educators. She encouraged BNSG/Wellesley women to participate in national professional associations, to form local clubs, to be active in the Mary Hemenway Alumnae Association, and to work toward a national association for all women physical educators.

Homans offered women physical educators a dual path to an active professional life. In 1909, the membership of the American Physical Education Association (APEA), formerly the AAAPE, numbered about 900.[1] Women had been present at the organizational meeting in 1885 and had participated in the association's regional and national meetings; however, only men had held the chief executive office. While Homans advised and encouraged women to join and be a part of the APEA, she saw the need for associations for women which would prepare them in decision-making, conducting meetings, presenting papers, and being comfortable and competent in professional situations. Homans never stated her ideas in these words, but her actions affirm this position.

With Homans' encouragement, the alumnae organized clubs in various cities and regions of the country. The name of these clubs, the Amy Morris Homans Club of ———, is a paradox in the almost faultless character which Homans presented to her students. Why this elderly dignified New England woman with extraordinarily high personal standards permitted her name to be used as the name of a club appears a mystery. One possible explanation is the fact that many women were more loyal to Homans than to BNSG or Wellesley. Perhaps, for this reason, Homans realized that the use of her name would draw alumnae together. She sensed the need for professional women to have social as well as professional outlets. Today, these clubs might be called support groups, but in the 1910s they were simply a means of drawing together Homans' former students.

The first club formed in Boston in 1916. Soon other clubs organized in cities such as New York, Philadelphia, and Atlanta. In the West, the clubs covered geographic areas such as central California and southern California. They met together, discussed problems, offered solutions to these problems, and enjoyed social occasions. The clubs reported their meetings and activities to Wellesley's annual *Bulletin* of the Department of Hygiene and Physical Education. There, women could read of the activities of their classmates, friends, and other alumnae.

Homans encouraged the alumnae to make gifts to Wellesley just as she had expected them to contribute to BNSG. On the occasion of Hemenway's death in 1894, she established the Alumnae Loan Fund, asking for a one-time pledge of 2 percent of one year's earnings if the alumna was making an adequate salary. The fund developed and was used to assist needy students. When Loretto Fish Carney '93, a loyal staff member, died suddenly in 1915, Homans again asked for alumnae contributions, hoping to reach the goal of $1,000.00. Finally, in 1920, she sent $1,081.00 to the Wellesley College treasurer to institute the Loretto Fish Carney Memorial Scholarship in 1921–1922.[2]

The Alumnae Association of BNSG became the Mary Hemenway Alumnae Association of Wellesley College. At the annual meeting at commencement time, Homans greeted the alumnae who had gathered and encouraged them in their work, inspiring them to strive for the high ideals she expounded for physical education for women. The alumnae came to appreciate Homans' standards and looked for ways to express their appreciation to her. Homans never encouraged students to know her informally or personally and maintained that posture when the students became alumnae. Her formal facade rarely displayed her emotions, which she kept tightly controlled, deep within herself. However, she held out to them her ideals of professional excellence and, as the years passed, accepted a certain homage such as the name of the local alumnae clubs. On the occasion of the 25th anniversary of BNSG, when the alumnae proposed to Homans that they have her portrait painted, she agreed. It is probable that she permitted the alumnae to undertake the project out of the mutual respect and high esteem she held for them individually and as a group.

In June, 1913, the alumnae commissioned Joseph deCamp to paint Homans' portrait as a gift from the Alumnae Association to the college. The association agreed to deCamp's fee of $3,000.00, but was unable to raise the entire amount by the time the portrait was finished and hung. Before the presentation of the portrait, the association paid deCamp $1,500.00 and continued its efforts to raise the money. In September, 1914, the artist received another $500.00, and then the association ran into serious difficulties. The 296 members of the Alumnae Association had contributed a total of $2,225.00, but had not been able to complete their pledges. With the approval of the executive committee, Helen McKinstry '00 approached Frederic Pratt of the Pratt Institute for assistance. McKinstry explained the circumstances to him:

Feeling assured of your interest in Physical Education, your respect for the School which has I believe graduated all the former and present women instructors of Physical Training at Pratt Institute, and your admiration and regard for the woman whose life work we have delighted to honor while yet she is here to be made glad by the tribute, even though by so doing an impecunious lot of women have been guilty of the very unbusiness like act of ordering a $3,000.00 portrait without visible means of paying for it,—I make bold to come to you for the assistance I am sure you will give us if you possibly can.[3]

Although the Alumnae Association had no security they offered over 25 signatures to promise to pay the $700.00 needed within five years if Pratt would loan the money to the associa-

Amy Morris Homans. *Portrait by Joseph deCamp,* 1913

tion. Pratt graciously complied and the association paid the deCamp bill in full. The alumnae returned $350.00 to Pratt in 1916 and the remainder the following year.[4]

In the portrait, Homans is quiety seated near a small table with a bowl of flowers. The charm and simplicity of the background, Homans' pose, attentive but not stiff, and her direct, serene gaze reminded her students of 25 years of the ideals that Homans represented. At the unveiling of the portrait, Mary Seeley Starks '99 gave an "Appreciation." She stressed Homans' special definition of womanliness and raised searching questions for the contemporary professional woman:

> The very most valuable quality of Miss Homans' character has been, through all the years, her womanliness. . . . And she not only showed us by example the finished product, a true woman, but she contrived to bring out in each girl with whom she came in contact her own latent powers of self-development.
>
> In these days of complicated living many puzzling problems beset us as women. . . . Are we suffragists, or are we not? . . . What is the relation of women to the cost of living? Are all women to become producers instead of conservers? And the relations of the sexes—on these and the countless other equally important subtopics of this great woman question we must have our views, and our views must and do reflect our ideals. . . . By what better means can we hope to solve them than by striving for that ideal held out to us here, the pursuit of womanliness? All round development of the individual, growth of character and of personality—these give promise for the future and a fresh answer to each new difficulty.[5]

By setting forth the ideal of Homans' *womanliness*—"the all round development of the individual, growth of character and of personality"—she supported ideas that did not place women in the usual passive feminine role. Homans favored her own definition of *womanliness*. For her, but not necessarily for others of the day, *womanliness* meant physical vigor, strength, and hard work by women with impeccable manners who were faultlessly groomed. The *womanliness* Homans supported made professional women acceptable members of society, yet permitted them to attain positions of power, leadership, and success.

For the alumnae, the portrait represented a tangible object which for many of them had a deep personal meaning. The fact that it took several years to complete the project made the effort very personal and the portrait more important to them. The portrait touched Homans and, just as she knew many details of their careers, she possibly knew of their difficulties in paying deCamp.

Following the formal unveiling of the portrait, the alumnae feted Homans at a dinner at the Wellesley Inn. For once, frivolity reigned. With Homans in a blue sunbonnet and Skarstrom in a black stovepipe hat, the alumnae donned all manner of caps, hats, and headgear. Surprises from bursting confetti bombs to awarding frying pans to the married women filled the evening. Elizabeth Wright '92 performed a skit on the early days of BNSG when it overlooked Boston's Granary Burying Ground. To everyone's delight, Homans, "to the meter of Hiawatha launched forth depicting with rare style the trials and tribulations of an artist's model."[6] The evening closed with the presentation of a pin to Homans, recognizing the 25th anniversary of BNSG.

As a group of professional women, Homans and her students had made great strides since the opening of BNSG in 1889. Homans encouraged the students from the BNSG and the early days at Wellesley to obtain an academic degree if they had not earned one before enrolling in the program. Early graduates who completed their degrees in medicine included Harriet Noyes Randall '93, J. Anna Norris and William Skarstrom '95, and Eleanor Mary Slater '96. Others who received academic degrees were Lillian Towne '91, B.A.; Mabel Cummings '97, B.S.; and Helen McKinstry '00, B.S. and M.A.

Following Homans' footsteps, some of the alumnae started their own schools of physical education which, in turn, helped spread Homans' ideals of women's physical education. The Boston School of Physical Education, founded in 1913 by three graduates of BNSG, was designed to meet the increasing demand for teachers of physical education. Incorporated in 1914, it listed among the members of the corporation Marguerite Sanderson '03, president; Mary F. Stratton '00, secretary-treasurer; and Marjorie Bouvé '03. The school, which moved to a permanent home in 1917, offered a two-year program and provided a camp experience for the students at the end of their second year. Such a school did not compete for students with Wellesley's program, and indeed, led to potential students who might complete a degree and apply to Wellesley.[7] In 1919 Helen McKinstry '00 founded the Central School of Hygiene and Physical Education in New York City.[8]

Homans continued her professional activities, attending the International Congress on Hygiene and Demography in Washington in 1912 and, a year later, giving a paper in Buffalo at the International Congress on Student Health. At Wellesley, with superb facilities available, Homans strengthened her ties with the alumnae through summer conferences. Here the alumnae could be brought up to date with the current theories in many specialties of physical education, become reacquainted with classmates, meet other alumnae, and maintain contact with Homans. The conferences served as another means of strengthening the professional community of women physical educators. In 1913, 80 alumnae attended a two-week summer conference from June 23 to July 19. They lived in College Hall and attended lectures and classes in gymnastics and dancing in Mary Hemenway Hall. They then took part in evening discussions in the students' parlor in College Hall. Skarstrom presented the latest theories and practice of gymnastics and Howe lectured on physiology. Dr. Joel E. Goldthwait spoke on posture and Franklin Fette explained methods of administering playgrounds. Dancing sessions completed each day, aesthetic dancing the first week and folk dancing the second week. In addition, many informal conversations and get-acquainted sessions took place. The alumnae expressed their appreciation to Homans for her efforts to provide them with the latest ideas in physical education.[9]

A national association for women in physical education had long been one of Homans' dreams and, during her first spring at Wellesley, she invited a group of physical education directors and the presidents of athletic associations to meet at Wellesley to discuss mutual problems. Homans held the meeting in Mary Hemenway Hall, where she could show her splendid new facility to her colleagues. Faculty from Bates, Colby, Mt. Holyoke, Radcliffe, and Smith attended.[10]

These same women and a few others met annually until, finally, in 1915, they organized the Association of Directors of Physical Education for Women. Homans believed the organization should be national and encouraged meetings outside New England. In 1916 the association met at Pratt Institute in New York and in 1917 at Randolph-Macon College in Lynchburg,

Virginia. In 1918, the year that Homans retired, they met at Smith College. Of the seventeen members present, ten were BNSG/Wellesley alumnae. Homans spoke to the group about the growing number of states requiring physical education in the public schools and the importance of physical education to the health of students entering colleges.[11] Homans continued to hope for a national professional women's physical education association, pressing certain alumnae to found such an organization.

Originally a peripheral, somewhat questionable gymnasium activity for men, physical education had now become acceptable at many colleges and universities. On many university campuses there were departments of physical education for women and, in the women's colleges, departments of physical education. At Wellesley, Homans had initiated a model graduate program in hygiene and physical education for women and, finally, she had taken steps to found a national association. From the need for gymnastics for Boston's school children, Homans had expanded her horizons to a future in which women fostered the ideals of health and vigor for the betterment of the citizenry of the country.

When Homans accepted a three-year appointment as professor of hygiene in 1915–1916, she agreed to retire upon the completion of the term. She would be 69 years old and, although she realized that much remained to be done, she believed she could now accomplish her goals through her students. Little is known about Homans' financial affairs, except that she had an excellent salary during her BNSG days and a small, lifetime annuity from the Hemenway estate. No mention is made of investments or private income from other sources. As her retirement approached, Wellesley sought to obtain a pension for her through the Carnegie Foundation. At the June 3, 1918, meeting of the Executive Committee of Wellesley's Board of Trustees, Pendleton announced that the pension had been refused, and recommended that Homans receive a grant of $1,500.00 (half salary) for the year 1918–1919 and the title of professor emeritus.[12] While the lack of pension created a problem in the future, Homans must have been pleased to be named professor emeritus of Wellesley College.

Homans retired as planned and, on June 15, 1918, over 120

alumnae and colleagues attended a luncheon in her honor. Maude Hopkins '91, Lillian Drew '93, William Skarstrom '95, Ruth Elliott '14, and Mabel Cummings '97 brought greetings from Boston, New York, the West, and the Midwest. The president of the Alumnae Association, Helen McKinstry '00, presented Homans with a wrist bag containing over $800.00 in Liberty Bonds, war-saving stamps, and thrift stamps. Then Homans spoke for the last time as director of the Wellesley program. Standing quietly in her usual dignified manner, in her familiar, well-modulated voice, she praised the past and looked into the future. She spoke of Hemenway's dream of better womanhood and her own stewardship of that dream, reminding her audience of the generous, loving woman who had created BNSG and foreseen the need to affiliate with a college such as Wellesley. Proud that the dream had been realized, Homans stressed the important step the department took in admitting only graduate students. She again noted Wellesley's need for a swimming pool and appointed a committee to begin raising money for that purpose. Speaking of the growing acceptance of physical education, Homans reminded her students that leadership positions awaited those who were prepared and that BNSG/Wellesley women should be active in the American Physical Education Association and help make it a success. Her remarks touched the alumnae who were charged with a "solidarity, and . . . a new vista of opportunity so that we may go forth to seek and win new distinction for our cause."[13]

At 69, still the epitome of professional womanhood, her oncoming deafness not yet too apparent, Homans disclosed some of her immediate plans. She hoped to travel, visit many of her former students, and make a study of hygiene and physical education in the United States, especially the women's programs.

12

Strengthening the Community of Women Physical Educators

After retirement, Homans chose to remain in Wellesley where her monument to Hemenway stood and where she could continue to visit with her students and assist the next director of hygiene and physical education at Wellesley. Her sister Trudy continued to make her home with her. They found a small apartment at 11 Appleby Road in Wellesley that Homans described as "flooded with sunshine, airy, and convenient." She wrote to Marion Watters Babcock '10 that "It does not seem little at all as we are three sides to the weather and plenty of windows. There is only one lack—a guest room. Nevertheless, we keep a couch in my sister's room to which I betake myself when there is a chance to have a friend with us."[1] Homans' income for this period is not known, other than the $800.00 annuity from the Hemenway estate. Savings and investments from earlier days may have provided an adequate living for the first years of her retirement.

Homans was offered at least two positions and accepted that of advisory director of the Central School of Hygiene and Physical Education, which was being established by Helen McKinstry '00 in New York City. As an advisor to McKinstry, Homans could live in Wellesley and visit the school in New York when necessary. Correspondence from Howe suggests that McKinstry may have created the position for her because she needed the money; however, there is no other evidence to substantiate this idea.[2] With the exception of moving to a smaller apartment, and somewhat simplifying her living, she appears to have conducted her life in much the same manner as before retirement.

Roxanne Vivian's appointment as Homans' successor surprised many people. She was neither an alumna of BNSG nor of Wellesley, and she was not a well-known physical educator. However, at least three reasons can be proffered to explain Vivian's selection. First, because of the many college and department changes made by Homans, the department needed an administrator rather than a leader with innovative ideas. Homans knew of Vivian's administrative abilities through the Women's Industrial Union in Boston. Not always friendly with all of her Wellesley colleagues, Homans did get along well with Vivian and could advise her easily, thus providing continuity in departmental affairs.

Second, Vivian, a professor of mathematics, held the Ph.D. degree, an essential for the newly approved graduate program in hygiene and physical education. Having secured graduate status for her program, Homans wished to ensure its success. Third, Homans had created a national network of BNSG/Wellesley women who were loyal to her. To have picked the next director from the alumnae—for example McKinstry, Trilling, Norris, or Perrin—might have divided the alumnae at a time when Homans believed they needed to work together. Some people referred to Vivian as Homans' shadow, and Vivian even explained some of her decisions with, "This is what Miss Homans feels we should do."[3]

Homans continued to lecture the new students on the necessity of being a "lady" in the Wellesley tradition. She socialized them into the emerging profession of physical education, making it quite clear that their professional future depended on proper conduct and excellent performance. Homans conducted these lectures until 1924 and, both before and after that time, entertained the graduate students in her home.

Carefully groomed, with hats and clean gloves, each fall the new students visited Homans and her sister. The students prepared to visit Homans with as much care as had the students of the early BNSG days. Rumors of Homans' standards of dress and deportment, as well as her reprimands, became part of the department lore, handed down from class to class. Homans' sister, known to the students as "Miss Gertrude," helped entertain them and put them at their ease. Homans, seated in her favorite chair, would ask each student, one at a time, to sit near her on a stool and then, due to increasing deafness, she would extend her ear trumpet, an old-fashioned hearing aid, toward the student. As if she was aware that many deaf people shouted, she asked her questions softly. The student riveted her attention on the carefully worded questions which had to be answered accurately and clearly. Homans inquired about the student's undergraduate college, her background, her interests, and her hopes for the future. Her keen insight and ability to estimate a student's success remained remarkable. Student reaction to these visits varied from professional anticipation of meeting a great pioneer in physical education to bored fulfillment of an assigned duty.

In keeping with the department tradition, the students remembered Homans' birthday with flowers and Homans sent notes of appreciation to the class. At the age of 76 she wrote to the first-year class, "It greatly pleases me that you should join the Senior Class in sending me such a gracious message with very beautiful roses on my birthday—seventy six must seem very old to you, but it is a very short time."[4] Not only was Homans pleased to become acquainted with the current students, but also she delighted in keeping in touch with her former students. She followed their careers with the same interest as she had before she retired. Now she traveled across the country to visit them, encouraging them and making suggestions as to the conduct of their work. During World War I she spoke proudly of the 48 BNSG/Wellesley physical education alumnae engaged in war service in the United States and Europe. Their posts included YWCA and YMCA programs, Red Cross responsibilities, and "reconstruction" or rehabilitation work in hospitals.[5] At times, Homans directed the alumnae's careers, advising them of positions available and of candidates for positions. She informed Mary-Ethel Ball '24 that she should apply for the position at the University of Colorado at Boulder and, then, wrote Clare Small '18, the director of the department, that "Mary-Ethel Ball will have written you. She wants to go home to Colorado. I talked with her and believe it is the very best place for her."[6] Another student, Elizabeth Abbott '24, recalled that Homans called her to her home and told her that "one of her girls" taught at Evanston Township High School, which had decided to appoint an additional woman physical education teacher. It had been decided that Abbott should go there and "it never occured to me not to go."[7]

Each year at the Wellesley Commencement, the alumnae gathered for a reunion and to welcome the graduating class as new alumnae. The occasion kept alive the history of BNSG/Wellesley, the benefits to be gained from physical education, the achievements of the alumnae, the goals Homans set for women in physical education, and the missionary zeal necessary to achieve these goals. In 1921, three years after her retirement, over 70 alumnae attended the reunion. The graduating students presented a "clever interpretation" of a student before entering Wellesley, after a month at Wellesley, and as a graduate. Songs and skits from the alumnae of the first class of 1891 to the class of 1916 followed. Homans then spoke, calling the members of the class of 1891 "pioneer women [who] had contributed to the realization of those ideals for which we must labor" and stressing the need of married alumnae to remain in close touch and be active in alumnae activities. She reminded the women of the importance of "our work to general education and the general scheme of a well rounded life." The class of 1910, the first Wellesley class, followed these inspirational remarks with a song dedicated to Homans:

> "H" is for the Heart which love has quickened.
> "O" is for the Only friend like her we know.
> "M" is for the Many times she's helped us.
> "A" at Any time when need we'd show.
> "N" is for the Numbers all who love her.
> "S" is every Single one that's here.
> 　　Put them all together they spell "Homans"—
> 　　The name that to our hearts is dear.[8]

At another reunion luncheon she reminded the alumnae that the larger aim of education was "the development of the whole man, body, mind, and spirit in perfect harmony." She inspired the students "so that when the day was over we went back to our families or work feeling not so far away in interest after all and most grateful for the years under her [Homans] leadership."[9]

Homans attended meetings of the Amy Morris Homans clubs across the country and spoke to the alumnae, usually on the importance of physical education for women. In 1925 Homans attended the meeting of the New York Amy Morris Homans Club and "gave one of her inspiring and friendly talks after which an opportunity was given to all the graduates to talk with her informally."[10] To others, she would point out the high ideals of the profession and instill in them a feeling that the alumnae had achieved these ideals.

In addition to meeting with the alumnae at reunions and meetings of the Amy Morris Homans clubs, Homans continued to call on them to make gifts to the department and to Wellesley. She initiated special funds, often beginning them with a personal contribution, and then soliciting the alumnae. While the amounts which the alumnae gave were never large, they served to reinforce the idea of a community of BNSG/Wellesley alumnae. A sum of $1,115.00 to be used for student loans was named the Maude G. Hopkins Fund after an early well-known BNSG graduate. Then the alumnae began a separate drive for $6,000.00 to establish an Amy Morris Homans Scholarship Fund. Augustus Hemenway, the son of Mary Hemenway, offered $3,000.00 if the alumnae could match that amount. Much to their satisfaction, the women raised the $3,000.00 by 1923.[11]

When Wellesley announced a special giving program for the Semi-Centennial Fund, Homans wrote to the alumnae stating that she had been "assured that all subscriptions from our alumnae will be credited to the Mary Hemenway Endowment Fund, now $100,700.00, the income of which is used only for salaries" and she urged alumnae to give even if the amount was very small.[12] The alumnae set a goal of $25,000.00 for the Semi-Centennial Fund.

To meet their goal, the women solicited large and small gifts, staged dances and other programs and created an annual Alumnae Sale. Homans enthusiastically supported this project and made every effort to make the sales successful. In 1925 the Alumnae Sale took place in the ballroom of the Wellesley Inn located in the center of Wellesley village. Amy Morris Homans clubs from all over the country sent delicacies. The Oregon women sent prunes and home-canned peaches, the Californians sent blanched almonds, walnuts, and orange blossom honey, and the Washingtonians contributed dried fruits and preserves. From New England were jellies, jams, and preserves. From Minnesota came 25-pound bags of flour; from Alaska, special curios; and from San Francisco's Chinatown, decorations. Other alumnae donated books and salable articles including scarfs, baked goods, handkerchiefs and lingerie. The graduate students made and sold candy. The fair generated such spirit that Florence (Johnson) Dunn '98 sent another $1,000.00. The alumnae had, by then, raised $16,200.00 of the $25,000.00 in less than three years.[13] The following year the annual sale raised $1,000.00 but, unlike the previous year, a considerable number of items were not sold. Homans took them home and sold them from her apartment, raising an additional $500.00.[14]

Projects to be funded by the Semi-Centennial Fund included a swimming pool, a facility which Homans supported enthusiastically. When BNSG moved to Wellesley, Homans had hoped for a swimming pool for the college and her program. As early as 1913 she had written, "It is regretted that we have no swimming pool. However, we hope to have one in the near future."[15] After the disastrous 1917 fire in College Hall, the Wellesley administration had asked Homans to support the Fire Fund rather than the Swimming Pool Fund. A hand-written note at the time of her retirement transferred $1,100.00 to Vivian to be used toward a swimming pool, as well as another sum of $3,382.46 which had accumulated from operating the college golf course, miscellaneous gifts to the department, and war bonds. At 82 she forwarded a check to Wellesley from Betty Lincoln, daughter of Mrs. Rachel H. Lincoln '96, marked "Good for the Fund."[16] Typical of women of the period with their small salaries, the alumnae slowly accumulated the amounts of their pledges. These efforts demonstrate Homans' enthusiasm and earnest attempts to raise money for Wellesley and her desire to improve the sport and recreational facilities for the college.

The feeling of community among the alumnae was enhanced by BNSG/Wellesley reunions at professional meetings. At 77,

Homans traveled to Rochester, New York, to attend the meetings of the Eastern District of the American Physical Education Association. There, she gave an inspirational talk to graduates of BNSG/Wellesley, the Central School of which Homans had been an advisory director, and the Boston School of Physical Education, established by BNSG alumnae.[17]

As Homans neared her 80th birthday, the alumnae made plans to make it a gala and memorable occasion. After months of careful preparation, the weekend of November 15 arrived. Homans received dozens of telegrams and other greetings. The Mary Hemenway Alumnae Association sent beautiful roses with a message that fresh flowers would arrive weekly for the remainder of her life. Ruth Elliott '14, the present director of the Department of Hygiene and Physical Education at Wellesley, arranged a birthday dinner for Homans and the faculty members of the department at the Wellesley College faculty club, followed by a reception for the graduate students.

On Saturday evening, November 17, the Amy Morris Homans Club of Boston honored Homans with a dinner party at the Parker House in Boston. Over 80 alumnae and friends attended. An extra place had been set at each table so that Homans could occupy the chair as she visited from table to table. The occasion was informal and happy as the alumnae chatted with Homans about the early days. One alumna described Homans that evening as "queenly in black velvet and fine old lace, looking . . . like a 'rare portrait by a master hand, radiating a personality which 80 years made more luminous and dominant.' "[18] There were no long formal speeches or programs and everyone enjoyed the party, Homans most of all.

Homans' most memorable birthday gift was a radio presented by the department at Wellesley and the faculty at the Central School in New York. The exciting equipment was installed in the Homans' apartment at a cost of $125.00 or $62.50 for each group.[19] The two sisters found great joy and satisfaction in this modern invention. Both quite deaf by this time, they fastened their ear trumpets to the radio and listed to music, drama, and, best of all, the news. Homans described her reactions to her 80th birthday as being "overwhelmed" by goodness, devotion, and a feeling of the old BNSG parties. She enjoyed meeting the graduate students and was delighted with her birthday cake, but she found her greatest joy in the radio. She particularly appreciated the variety of programs offered by the modern instrument, but noted that she chose not to listen to jazz.[20]

The following June, 1929, the Department of Hygiene and Physical Education celebrated the 40th anniversary of BNSG. Homans agreed to address the group on the history of the school. Clear, perceptive, and looking ahead, she spoke of the original values Hemenway had envisioned and the need to amplify them for the future. She explained the unique role of the teacher of physical education in the life of the student and justified her insistence on the highest standards for BNSG/Wellesley students. Always the faithful disciple, Homans did not let the alumnae and students in 1929 forget that it was Mary Hemenway to whom they paid tribute and owed the founding of the school. She spoke with satisfaction of the work of her graduates and, in turn, the women they had educated, referring to this process as "an endless chain" which she hoped would continue to inspire future generations of teachers.[21]

Several years earlier Homans had received one of the highest honors in physical education, election to the American Academy of Physical Education. In 1926, five well-known physical educators, Clark W. Hetherington, R. Tait McKenzie, William Burdick, Thomas Storey, and Jay B. Nash, founded the academy to honor outstanding men and women physical educators and to advance the field of physical education. The founders decided that, in the future, all new members, or "fellows," must be unanimously chosen by the present members.[22] These five men then "elected" five additional physical educators including one woman, Jessie Bancroft. At the second meeting in 1927, five more fellows were added, including Amy Morris Homans, the second woman elected to the group. This honor attests to the esteem in which Homans was held by her professional colleagues.

Still keenly interested in life, especially the professional careers and the continuing achievements of her students, Homans faced an increasing number of troubling physical problems. She recovered from a gall bladder operation, but arthritis, minor ailments, and increasing deafness gradually isolated her from many facets of life. Not only did Homans require an ear trumpet by this time, but her vision grew dim. Loyal students continued to visit her, trying to use the ear trumpet as if they were accustomed to it. In spite of these difficulties, Homans maintained an illusion of perfection that had been characteristic of her professional and personal life. Former students, many of them now well-known professional women in their own right, helped maintain this illusion. Fortunately, Homans' mind remained keen. She had a lively interest in American education and physical education, questioning all her visitors about contemporary issues.

13

The Final Touches

Homans' last years brought the realization of two long-time hopes: a national association for women in physical education, and deserved recognition for herself by professional colleagues. Much to Homans' satisfaction, in 1924 the three district associations of college directors of physical education for women finally formed a national association. The fact that the organizing committee—Mabel Cummings '97 from Wellesley, J. Anna Norris '95 from Minnesota, and Helen Bunting '12 from Stanford—were all BNSG/Wellesley alumnae indicates the leadership of Homans' students in achieving this goal.[1] As one of its first acts, and in recognition of her leadership, the group named Amy Morris Homans an honorary member.[2]

In February, 1929, *The Sportswoman*, a journal dedicated to the advancement of sport for women, carried a tribute to Homans. Prepared by Fannie Garrison '03, it briefly traced the beginning of BNSG, stressing Homans' emphasis on high standards and excellence in all things and at all times. "She impressed on her students a professional attitude toward their work—they must be dignified in appearance and manner, they must be thorough students, combining theory and practice when only the latter was stressed, they must regard their work as part of one great whole and that whole education in its broadest sense."[3] The tribute stressed the strong social purpose of physical education as a profession rather than an occupation.

The next two years brought further honors. In June, 1930, Russell Sage College awarded honorary doctorate degrees to

Amy Morris Homans, Florence Gibb Pratt, and Eva Le-Gallienne.[4] Pratt, the first woman regent of the University of New York, was recognized for her accomplishments in education and the state government, and LeGallienne for her "outstanding achievements on the American stage." Homans' citation called her an "educational pioneer and mother of the modern program of Physical Education for women in America."[5]

The following year Homans received an Honor Award from the American Physical Education Association (APEA). The occasion proved both happy and sad for Homans and her students. Delighted by the selection of Homans, her former students were dismayed to discover that financial difficulties might prevent her from making the trip to Detroit, Michigan, to receive the honor. Marion Watters Babcock '10, who over the years had become a close friend of Homans and knew what inroads the Depression had made on her resources, doubted if Homans could afford the trip. At that time Mabel Lee '10, president of APEA and a close friend of Babcock, initiated plans to make it possible for Homans to make the trip. Babcock offered to escort Homans to Detroit and to assist her while she was there.

Lee proposed that a group of Homans' students invite her to come to Detroit as their guest and, in addition to attending the Honor Award ceremony, invite her to be the guest of honor at a Wellesley luncheon. Lee asked for the opinion of Ruth Elliott '14, the present head of the department at Wellesley. Did she think Homans would accept such an invitation? What Midwest alumna could take on the responsibility of such a venture? She reminded Elliott that:

Miss Homans has never attended a convention in the Middle west and it will be a great treat to have her come. She is an honorary member of all three groups meeting: the Director's Society in Ann Arbor, the W.D. [Women's Division] of the N.A.A.F. [National Amateur Athletic Federation] in Detroit on Tues. and Wed., and the A.P.E.A. the rest of the week. It will be wonderful to have her there in person to receive her honor award.[6]

Elliott replied immediately agreeing in part with Lee's proposals, but suggesting some modifications. She believed that

Homans was in excellent health and would enjoy the visit to Detroit. She suggested, though, that a general appeal to the alumnae would be inappropriate for two reasons. First, Homans would find it distasteful. Second, an appeal was already being made to the alumnae for a gift for Skarstrom on his retirement in June, 1931. Elliott enclosed her check for $10.00 and offered to contribute more if necessary. She thought the idea of having "the Mid-west group invite Miss Homans as their guest an excellent one."[7]

They agreed to contact a few alumnae and, finally, sixteen BNSG alumnae, all directors of physical education, contributed to the expenses of Homans' Detroit trip. Babcock accompanied her. To everyone's surprise and pleasure, Lee, as the president of APEA, was assigned a suite of rooms in the hotel. This enabled Homans to occupy a small bedroom in the suite and have the comfort of a living room in which to receive guests.[8]

The Honor Award ceremony, a highlight of the APEA convention, took place at the opening meeting. Lee, the first woman president of APEA, presided and announced that the APEA had adopted the policy of honoring "individuals for meritorious service in the profession of physical education or in allied fields of science and education by electing such persons as 'Fellows of the American Physical Education Association.'" She pointed out that, because it was the first time the association had honored any of its members, there would be a number of awards.

Amy Morris Homans, then 82 years of age, received the first award. Standing erect, smiling, too deaf to hear every word of the recognition and praise accorded her, Homans listened as her former student, Mabel Lee, read her citation:

Miss Homans is professor emeritus of physical education at Wellesley College. Her early labors on behalf of physical education were given to the development of the Boston Normal School of Gymnastics which later through the efforts of Miss Homans became the department of hygiene and physical education at Wellesley. An army of leaders with the ideals and love of their profession at heart has been Miss Homans' contribution. A work well done and reaping its reward a hundred-fold.[9]

As the audience rose to give her an ovation, Homans smiled in quiet appreciation.

In addition to Homans, four alumnae of BNSG and a member of the Wellesley College faculty received awards. Among the honorees were Ethel Perrin '92, J. Anna Norris '95, Lydia Clark '08, and Blanche Trilling '09, and Eugene Howe of the Wellesley College faculty. Homans must have been pleased that she was recognized, but even more pleased that her students were honored. They were all administrators—Clark at the University of California, Berkeley; Norris at the University of Minnesota; and Trilling at the University of Wisconsin. Perrin directed public school physical education in Detroit, Michigan. Not all of the first group of honorees could be present in Detroit and, a few weeks later at the meeting of the Eastern District, Skarstrom '95 received his citation.[10]

Homans returned to Wellesley with her spirits buoyed up and looking forward with mixed emotions to "Billy" Skarstrom's retirement ceremonies in June. The Wellesley faculty, the department faculty, alumnae, graduate students, and Homans honored "Docky," as the students affectionately called him, with tributes of praise, gifts, and a purse. Homans' tribute expressed her feelings for Skarstrom:

> Dr. William Skarstrom, proud father of an able, scholarly son;
> Dr. Skarstrom, an ardent lover of his profession;
> Dr. Skarstrom, the beloved, devoted friend of us all;
> William Skarstrom, the Christian gentleman;
>   We salute you.[11]

For Homans, the occasion was another moment in the realization of an era drawing to a close.

While her life overflowed with outward recognition of her achievements, her personal life became more and more austere. Financial problems now plagued Homans and her sister. It can be postulated that Homans' resources, which might have been adequate at the time of her retirement, diminished greatly after the crash of 1929. The Homans sisters lived simply, limited their menus, and reduced their housekeeper's hours to one half-day every other week. Homans attempted to resign from the American Academy of Physical Education, but was not permitted to relinquish this honor. When she received a letter sent

to all members of the Academy soliciting funds to assist in publishing Clark W. Hetherington's work, Homans wrote to Jay B.
Nash that "my funds are so depleted by the depression that I
cannot make a contribution."[12]

Although the situation must have been distasteful to her,
gradually Homans accepted support from her former students.
Her circle of intimate friends and confidants grew smaller and
she appeared to lean more on a few of her former students.
Babcock became a trusted friend and came to visit from her
home in Philadelphia as often as possible. She provided a willing ear for the aging Homans who talked about "her hopes for
women educated in the profession," "the importance of studying for the Ph.D. degree," and about facing her personal problems "with a sense of humor and laughter." She even disclosed
her recipe for home-brewed wine made from cherries, raisins,
yeast, and water. Babcock found that Homans continued to inspire people. Once after returning to Philadelphia she confided
that Homans had "recharged my spiritual storage batteries and
that I could go better and stronger for her influence."[13] Helen
McKinstry '00 added much to Homans' comfort in these years.
She visited Homans and her sister, took them on excursions in
New England, provided some financial help, and assisted in
whatever way she could.

In April, 1933, Homans fell ill, possibly as a result of a stroke,
and remained bedridden for the final months of her life. During the early weeks of her illness, Homans expected to recover.
Unable to attend the annual dinner and meeting of the Mary
Hemenway Alumnae Association on June 16 at Wellesley, she
sent Miss Gertrude to represent her and also wrote a personal
message to the alumnae:

Will you tell the Alumnae that I have been incapacitated for ten weeks?
The muscles of my feet and legs had grown, during my 84 years,
somewhat weakened and refused to do any work. So I have spent the
10 weeks in bed resting them. They have grown almost quite strong
again, and had the meeting been two weeks later, there is no doubt
but what I should have been present. I am learning to walk, and get-
ting along a good deal faster than it was expected that I would. In every
other way I am perfectly well except for the handicaps of not seeing
and not hearing, but I do not mind them.[14]

As Homans grew weaker, her need for nursing care increased, further straining the meager resources of the sisters. Finally, in September, McKinstry wrote to Wellesley faculty member Fanny Garrison '03, revealing Homans' financial plight and suggesting an appeal to the alumnae. She also offered to write to the Hemenway family to request additional funds for Homans.

By October, Homans began to fail rapidly. She apparently did not suffer, but often could not recognize those around her. With still more nursing care required, the Alumnae Association took immediate action to assist with the increased costs. The "Flower Fund" that had provided weekly fresh flowers for Homans since her 80th birthday had a balance of $301.41. The committee in charge withdrew $250.00 and sent it to Miss Gertrude. Typical of the relationship between the alumnae and Homans, the committee retained a small amount so they could continue to send Homans the weekly flowers.[15]

A special committee consisting of Fanny Garrison '03, Edith Sears '98, Margaret Johnson '03, Harriet Clarke '28, and Ruth Elliott '14 was appointed to deal with Homans' financial problems. The committee planned to initiate a gift-giving project for Homans' 85th birthday and proposed that a gift of money would be most appropriate. They solicited all alumnae who had graduated prior to 1930. Elliott sent personal appeals to Marion Watters Babcock '10, Josephine Rathbone Karpovich '22, Mary Coleman '10, Mabel Lee '10, Elizabeth Halsey '16, J. Anna Norris '95, Violet Marshall '14, and Blanche Trilling '09.[16] Homans' financial situation continued to surprise the alumnae who did not know the facts. They responded to the appeal immediately, revealing their great concern for Homans and also reflecting their own struggle with life during the Depression. Many of these women faced reduced salaries and additional family responsibilities from aging parents. Their gifts were small and usually accompanied with a wish that the amount could have been larger. These women contacted other alumnae. In all, over 200 BNSG/Wellesley alumnae came to Homans' aid. Their gifts varied from $1.00 to $25.00, but together they totaled $1,113.00.[17]

Homans never knew of her students' efforts in her own behalf. On Sunday morning, October 29, 1933, she quietly died in her sleep. Babcock and McKinstry came to Wellesley and, with Elliott, did what they could to assist Miss Gertrude. Funeral services were announced for St. Andrews Episcopal Church in Wellesley, but, unknown to Miss Gertrude, Homans had made special arrangements to have a private service at home for only the family. Elliott, McKinstry, and Babcock, aware that the newspaper announced services at the church, gathered there and were joined by a few others including a member of the Hemenway family. After performing the private service requested by Homans, the minister returned to the forlorn few at the church and read a prayer for the solace of those who had come to pay homage to Amy Morris Homans.[18]

The $1,100.00 collected by the alumnae was presented to Miss Gertrude, who accepted it gratefully and with deep appreciation.[19] After a few weeks in Wellesley, she returned to Vassalboro, Maine, the village where she and her sister had spent their childhood. She continued to keep in touch with those alumnae who had been close to Homans in her last years.

As news of Homans' death became known, tributes poured in extolling Homans' achievements and her influence on physical education, on her students, and on the profession of physical education for women. Skarstrom, an alumnus, Wellesley faculty member, and personal friend, expressed the thoughts of many:

A great and noble, valiant spirit has passed from us. . . . Her influence on my career, my whole life, was great and always for my good. And I believe that is true of hundreds of others . . . Her ideals of life and work . . . put their stamp on most of the graduates whose training she directed, and through time, has permeated in considerable measure to the physical education profession.[20]

The Eastern District Association of the APEA praised her contributions to physical education in the United States:

To those who were privileged to know her either professionally or personally, her vision and indomitable courage, her sense of justice, and her great womanliness and charm typified the best in leadership. She was an example of the finest in professional womanhood. Her great spirit still leads on in the profession she so largely helped to create, and which she ennobled and dignified.[21]

The National Association of Directors of Physical Education for Women in Colleges and Universities, founded by Homans, passed a resolution acknowledging the "power of her spirit" and the "structure of influence" which will continue. The resolution concluded, "Everyone of us, directly or indirectly, has been enriched by the dignity given to our work by her life. It would be her wish to have each of us feel that Amy Morris Homans is still her friend."[22]

After Wellesley College terminated the professional program in physical education in 1953, Homans' name and accomplishments seemed to fade as a central figure in the history of physical education and professional education for women. However, as interest in women's history revived in the 1960s, Homans' early leadership was recognized with a lecture series sponsored by the National Association for Physical Education of College Women.[23] Here "the third and fourth generations" of BNSG/Wellesley alumnae honored the founder of their organization. Mabel Lee '10, who had presented Homans the APEA Honor Award in 1931, gave the tribute at the inaugural lecture. She described Homans as a benevolent autocrat and recalled her faith in the development of physical education for women as a profession. Lee characterized her as a "woman of dynamic personality, of high courage, unflinching in maintenance of high standards, inexorable in her insistence upon the pursuit of professional excellence—yet a woman who claimed the deep respect, sincere admiration and devoted homage of her students."[24]

It is now almost a century since Hemenway and Homans began their pursuit of improving the health of the country through "bodily education." Homans expanded this idea, pioneered professional education for women, and molded a profession for women. Homans' story is one of sustained belief in the ability of women to benefit from exercise and sport, to create a profession, and to be leaders in that profession.

14

Epilogue

In 1929, at the annual meeting of the Mary Hemenway Alumnae Association at Wellesley, Amy Morris Homans, age 80, recounted her perceptions of the importance of physical education, commending BNSG's founder, Mary Hemenway, and quietly but modestly paying tribute to her own achievements:

From the outset we saw the need of something which would lift the life of the masses to a higher level of health and vigor, to a more sane and wholesome outlook, a more rational, self-controlled way of living. The comparatively new field of hygiene and physical education seemed more promising in these directions than anything else. I am more than ever convinced that the choice was a wise one. For in the activities of physical education the young human reveals and expresses his fundamental self perhaps more truly and more completely than in any other way.

. . . It is a great satisfaction to see the good work go on in "the third and fourth generation" of teachers trained by our graduates, and their graduates in turn, an endless chain, and I hope that the old school will always be known for its high standards and the quality of its product and that it will remain a living spring and constant source of inspiration to generations of teachers yet unborn.[1]

By 1929 when she made these remarks, Homans' "endless chain" did, indeed, exist. At the time of her retirement, 344 of the 677 living graduates of BNSG/Wellesley were active in physical education. Of these, 105 taught in normal schools, colleges, and universities in many parts of the country.[2] Particularly in institutions with physical education majors, these alumnae instructed more and more women in Homans' ideals and standards. Even in the 1980s, professional physical education students can trace members of their faculty and administration back to Homans. For Homans, in 1929, looking far into the future, today's students represented those "generations of teachers yet unborn."

Proudly and affectionately, Homans referred to "the old school" and praised its "high standards" and "the quality of its product," both reflecting the success of her efforts. Her criteria of high standards and quality had become the hallmarks of Homans as an educator. Stressing the desire to improve the lives of the average American through a selected regimen of exercise and physical activities, Homans did not couch her remarks in the narrow terms of her original curriculum of Swedish gymnastics, but instead employed the broad conception of "activities of physical education," testifying to the inclusion of many forms of play, exercise, dance, and sport in the curriculum of the late 1920s. She appeared satisfied with her life's work and praised her former students for their good work and for creating "the third and fourth generation" of teachers trained by BNSG/Wellesley alumnae. Her forward-looking comments recognized the many changes which had taken place in the forty years of her career in physical education.

When BNSG opened, Homans battled nineteenth-century views that the rigors and study necessary in higher education would sap women of the strength intended to develop their reproductive systems, that women were mentally and physiologically inferior to men, that vigorous exercise and sport might render women masculine, and that women should remain in the home or accept positions closely aligned to homemaking. By the late 1920s, young women no longer quaked under the threats of E. H. Clarke's gloomy predictions that college study would damage their reproductive organs and that they would not be able to perform their womanly functions. Research and experience proved that menstruation and childbearing should be considered normal functions of the female body, and that physical activity such as exercise and sport did not interfere with these functions.

Homans and her students, along with many other physical educators and reformers, can be credited with helping to institute the concept that regular exercise and sport increases the vigor of women and improves their health. They also insisted on appropriate clothing for exercise. While "appropriate" in the 1890s meant heavy bloomers, women did rid themselves of tight corsets, voluminous petticoats, and floor-length skirts for exercise. Slowly women adopted sport clothing which permitted greater freedom of body movement. In the 1920s, when women's street dresses suddenly became knee-length, women's sport clothing changed to knickers, shorts, and brief swim suits.

In the Roaring Twenties women not only wore knee-length dresses and shorts, but they also bobbed their hair, smoked in public, and became sport stars. Gertrude Ederle bettered the men's record when she swam the English Channel and tennis star Helen Wills acquired the nickname "Queen of the Nets." M. K. Constance Applebee of Bryn Mawr College opened her hockey camp for women and girls in 1922. In addition to these sports, women bowled, bicycled, rode horseback, fenced, rowed, and played basketball and many other sports. Despite the apparent increase in women's sport in the 1920s, many old beliefs lingered. In the 1928 Olympic Games when athletic or track and field events for women were held for the first time, some contestants "staggered" across the finish line, reviving the old arguments that strenuous sport might harm women.

Homans and her students decried public scenes which placed women's sport in such an unfavorable light and, indeed, shunned the world of the sport star. Women physical educators, influenced by Homans, endeavored to create an atmosphere in which sport for women would be unquestioned. They defined women's sport as different than men's sport with the hope that sport programs designed especially for women would be seen as feminine and, therefore, acceptable. They avoided copying the men's current athletic programs which the women identified with the growing commercialism and professionalism of intercollegiate athletics, especially football. In contrast to men's athletics, the women perceived varsity teams, spectators, and publicity as unnecessary in women's sport. From the beginning they favored strenuous exercise and physical activity for all women, but always within the socially acceptable parameters of womanhood. This philosophy, while never denying competition, did not condone competitive and championship programs which might drain the meager budgets usually assigned to women, thus excluding the average woman from exercise and sport. The programs developed by Homans and her students promoted health and vigor for all women, a wide range of exercise, sport, and dance activities, women teachers for girls and women, and the ideals of amateurism. They taught generations of women to exercise and play, which, in part, led to the explosion of women's sport in the 1960s and 1970s.

A careful analysis of Homans' career clearly shows that from 1889 to 1924 Homans molded physical education for women into a profession. At a time when nurses acquired their skills in an apprenticeship and training for careers in social work did not yet exist, Homans took the necessary steps to initiate a profession for women. Seizing every opportunity available and creating others as necessary, Homans met the criteria ascribed to today's definition of a profession.[3] First, she promoted physical education as a means of benefiting the community by bettering the health and vigor of the citizenry.

Her 1929 remarks, in which she noted that "in the activities of physical education the young human reveals and expresses his fundamental self . . . more truly and more completely than in any other way," reveal her broad conceptual approach to physical education. Homans considered physical education as "human race culture" and part of the American dream of "the good life." From her early years in physical education, when she spoke of bettering womanhood, to her address in honor of the BNSG/Wellesley program's 40th anniversary, Homans used the generalizations of an educational theorist whose aim was to benefit society.

Homans fulfilled the second criterion of a profession, the development of philosophical positions to guide the conduct of the profession and its members, through the curricular and the extracurricular experiences provided for the students. Homans believed that the teacher of physical education accepted the role of being a model for students and should impart the place of physical education in "the good life" by example. Homans acted as model for her students and she expected her alumnae to do the same. At both BNSG and Wellesley, Homans counseled the students, dwelling on points which helped formulate their professional philosophical positions.

Homans' interest in the third criterion of a profession, adding to the knowledge of the field, was evident as early as the 1889 Conference in the Interest of Physical Training. In the early years, with little material published for students to study, Homans relied on the sciences basic to the study of the human body and exercise. She obtained faculty from Harvard University and MIT to teach the sciences and appointed highly qualified faculty in gymnastics, dance, and sport. She was a forerunner in incorporating sports such as basketball, swimming, and field hockey into the curriculum.

When BNSG opened, little literature in the field existed. In 1889 Hemenway privately published the *Report of the Conference in the Interest of Physical Training* and, in 1893, assisted Sweden's Royal Central Institute of Gymnastics to publish some of the Ling gymnastic drawings. Homans continued the practice of publishing papers and pamphlets prepared by the faculty and alumnae, thus adding to the literature of physical education. At Wellesley, research and publication became even more important as Homans planned for a graduate program. Although Homans presented papers at only a few professional meetings and published little, she expected her faculty and her alumnae to advance the emerging field of physical education.

The fourth criterion for a profession is the establishment of qualifications, attitudes, and ethical behaviors appropriate to the profession and the promotion of a sense of community among its members. Homans realized that women in physical education had to overcome the public's preconceptions about women in a professional field which dealt with exercise and sport, to women in graduate work, and to women in administrative positions. Homans prepared her students to overcome these objections and inculcated in them the need for womanly, professional appearance and behavior. Despite her stern, sometimes repressive tactics, she instilled confidence and self-worth in her students.

Homans created a strong sense of community among her alumnae and, later, encouraged a sense of community among all women in physical education. First at BNSG, and then at Wellesley, she initiated alumnae associations and other activities including fund-raising. Never implying that the women should make large contributions to any one project, she expected each woman to give what she could to support the program. After the move to Wellesley, Homans expected the BNSG graduates to contribute to the college and always included them in her efforts to raise money. Each year at the time of Wellesley's commencement, the annual meeting of the Mary Hemenway Alumnae Association brought Homans' former students together. Tradition reigned as the graduating class met the alumnae and become part of that association. In what might appear an aberration from her stern, aloof demeanor, Homans allowed her alumnae to identify with her in certain controlled ways. The portrait of Homans painted in 1913 serves as one example. She also permitted her name to be used for clubs which brought the alumnae together for professional and social purposes.

While these associations strengthened alumnae ties, Homans promoted a larger sense of community among all women physical educators. From 1910 to 1915 she convened women directors of physical education in colleges and, when she thought the women ready, formed the Association of Directors of Physical Education for Women in the East. She constantly prompted her students to organize similar associations in other parts of the country, with the purpose of combining later into one national association. In 1924, Homans' dream of a national association of women in physical education finally became a reality. When Lydia Clark '08 became the association's first president, one can imagine the pleasure it brought Homans. While Homans did not have clearly defined criteria to follow, her work in the pioneering days of women's professional education demonstrates clearly that she created a profession for women.

Homans also succeeded in the final thrust of her work, educating women for positions of leadership and authority. The unique professional preparation of her graduates made them sought after by college and university presidents. BNSG and Wellesley alumnae occupied positions in many prestigious women's colleges and state universities across the country and in several foreign countries. As leadership positions opened to women in the American Physical Education Association, Homans' students filled them. Berenson '92 chaired the first women's basketball rules committee, and others were active in the development of a variety of women's sports. BNSG/Wellesley alumnae became the first women presidents in the district associations and, in 1931, Mabel Lee '10 became the first woman president of the national association. Also, BNSG/Wellesley alumnae emerged as leaders at the 1923 landmark Conference on Athletics and Physical Education for Women and Girls in Washington, D.C. In professional associations and on campuses across the country, Homans' students made their mark. They held many offices and leadership positions in associations and contributed to the development of colleges and universities. They founded schools and have had buildings, gymnasiums, and athletic fields named in their honor.

Amy Morris Homans' life spanned eight decades—from the mid-nineteenth century before the Civil War to the Depression of the 1930s. In the late-nineteenth century, work, education, and the professions gradually opened new opportunities for women and created the need for professional education for women. Homans, a self-educated and very able woman, pioneered professional education for women in the emerging field of physical education. The remarkable Miss Homans dedicated her life to bettering the condition of women through exercise, sport, dance, and physical activities and to educating women to be leaders in a professional field. Her story adds to the understanding of the early pioneers in women's education, the many obstacles which they overcame, and their achievements.

Notes

ABBREVIATIONS USED IN NOTES

BNSG: Boston Normal School of Gymnastics

CBNSG: *Catalogue*, Boston Normal School of Gymnastics

DHPE: Department of Hygiene and Physical Education, Wellesley College, Wellesley, MA

LTR: *The Lighthouse and Tileston Recorder*, newspaper published by the Tileston Normal School, Wilmington, NC. c. 1872–1886

MHAAB: *Bulletin*, Mary Hemenway Alumnae Association, Graduate Department of Hygiene and Physical Education, Wellesley College

Phillips Library: Peabody Museum of Salem, Salem, MA

Robinson: Elmo A. Robinson and Eugene C. Howe, "Amy Morris Homans," c.1940, 3P Amy Homans, Wellesley College Archives

WCA: Wellesley College Archives

Scrapbook: Scrapbooks on Health and Gymnastics in America, I (1889–1893); II (1900–1903); III (1889–1894); DHPE: BNSG, WCA

WCB: Wellesley College *Bulletin*, WCA

Alumnae information is found in the 1961 *Register*, Hygiene and Physical Education, Wellesley College and Boston Normal School of Gymnastics, WCA. BNSG/Wellesley graduates are cited in the text and notes by class numerals immediately following the name, Jane Doe 'xx. When a name appears frequently, the numerals are omitted after the first reference to that person. Anecdotes and information reported by several alumnae are not footnoted.

1: PROLOGUE

1. See among others Everett C. Hughes, "Professions," and Bernard Barber, "Some Problems in the Sociology of Professions," in *The

Professions in America, ed. Kenneth S. Lynn (Boston: Houghton Mifflin, 1965), pp. 1–14, 15–34; Wilbert E. Moore, *The Professions: Roles and Rules* (New York: Russell Sage Foundation, 1970); Eliot Freidson, *Profession of Medicine* (New York: Dodd, Mead, 1970), Ch. 4; and William J. Goode, "Community within a Community: The Professions," *American Sociological Review* 22 (April 1957): 194–200.

2. Rudolph C. Blitz, "Women in the Professions, 1870–1970," *Monthly Labor Review* 97 (May 1974): 35–39.

3. Normal school: Early school of one or two years designed to train teachers. In the nineteenth century many normal schools were private institutions that did not grant degrees, but offered post secondary studies which qualified students for a teaching license. By the mid-twentieth century, most normal schools had become state institutions with a four-year curriculum leading to a bachelor's degree.

4. Thomas Woody, *A History of Women's Education in the United States* (New York: Science Press, 1929), 2, p. 75.

5. *Encyclopedia of Library and Information Science* (New York: Marcel Dekker, 1972), 7, p. 418.

6. Personal interview with Marion Watters Babcock '10, May, 1968.

7. "Early Recollection of Homans by Senior Faculty Members," History: General (1882–1946): Folder II, 3L DHPE, WCA.

8. Robinson, p. 1.

9. Margery Taylor '39, "An Historical Study of Professional Training in Hygiene and Physical Education in the Boston Normal School of Gymnastics and Wellesley College," Seminar Paper, Wellesley College, 1938, WCA.

10. William Skarstrom '95, "Life and Work of Amy Morris Homans," in *Pioneer Women in Physical Education, Supplement to the Research Quarterly* 12 (October 1941): 615–627.

11. Mary Hemenway Hall was razed in 1984. All materials are now housed in the Wellesley College Archives (WCA).

12. *Pioneer Women in Physical Education*, Foreword.

13. *Pioneer Women in Physical Education*.

2: FROM COUNTRY SCHOOL TEACHER TO BOSTON REFORMER

1. William Skarstrom, "Life and Work of Amy Morris Homans," in *Pioneer Women in Physical Education, Supplement to the Research Quarterly* 12 (October 1941): 615–627.

2. Town Report, March 31, 1865, Vassalboro, ME, the Vassalboro Historical Society, Vassalboro, ME.

3. See among others Walter L. Fleming, *Documentary History of Re-*

construction (Cleveland: Clark, 1907), 2, pp. 165–168; and Henry Lee Swint, *The Northern Teacher in the South: 1862–1870* (New York: Octagon Books, 1967).

4. "The Wilmington Mission," LTR, January 9, 1872.

5. Charles Lowe, "Miss Amy M. Bradley, and Her Schools in Wilmington, N.C.," *Old and New* 1 (June 1870): 775–779.

6. Martin to Bradley, August 18, 1870, Board of Education, Wilmington, NC.

7. See Chapter 1, No. 3.

8. Rose Geranium, "Mrs. Hemenway and Our School," LTR, May 14, 1872.

9. Elisabeth M. Herlihy, ed., *Fifty Years of Boston: A Memorial Volume* (Boston: Tercentenary Committee, 1932).

10. William A. Leahy, "The Population," in Herlihy, p. 67.

11. Leahy, p. 69.

12. See among others Arthur Mann, *Yankee Reformers in the Urban Age* (Cambridge: Harvard University, 1954), esp. Ch. 4, "Protestant Gospels of Social Redemption"; Barbara M. Solomon, *Ancestors and Immigrants* (Cambridge: Harvard University, 1956); and Nathan I. Huggins, *Protestants Against Poverty* (Westport, CT: Greenwood, 1971).

13. Betty Spears, "The Building Up of Character Has Been My Aim," *Journal of Health, Physical Education, and Recreation* 42 (March 1971): 93–94.

14. Edison to Lathrop, May 25, 1888, Phillips Library.

15. Newspaper clippings, Old South Papers, Boston Athenaeum, Boston, MA.

16. LTR, October 1884.

17. Charles Gordon Ames, A Memorial Service, Church of the Disciples, March 11, 1894, p. 19.

18. John O. Norris, "Address," in *Memorial Services in Honor of Mrs. Mary Hemenway*, ed. Larkin Dunton (Boston: 1914), pp. 84–85.

19. "A Message from Miss Homans," MHAAB, September 1929, p. 3.

20. See among others E. H. Clarke, *Sex in Education; or, a Fair Chance for Girls* (Boston: Houghton Mifflin, 1873); D. A. Sargent, "The Physical Development of Women," *Scribner's Magazine* 5 (February 1889): 172–185; G. S. Hall, *Adolescence* (New York: Appleton, 1904); and Mary Putnam Jacobi, *The Question of Rest for Women During Menstruation* (New York: G. P. Putnam, 1877).

21. Clarke, p. 59.

22. Clarke, pp. 85–87, 103.

23. M. Carey Thomas, "Present Tendencies in Women's Colleges and University Education," *Educational Review* (1908): 69.

24. Scrapbook I, p. 5.

25. M. L. Rayne, *What Can a Woman Do?* (Peterburgh, NY: Eagle, 1893), p. 22.

26. See among others Betty Spears and Richard A. Swanson, *History of Sport and Physical Activity in the United States*, 2d ed. (Dubuque, IA: Wm. C. Brown, 1983).

27. Arabella Kenealy, "Woman as Athlete," *The Nineteenth Century* 266 (1899): 636–645.

3: VICTORIAN VIEWS OF EXERCISE

1. For more detailed information on these developments, see among others Spears and Swanson; Fred Eugene Leonard and R. Tait McKenzie, *History of Physical Education* (Philadelphia: Lea & Febiger, 1923); Ellen W. Gerber, *Innovators and Institutions in Physical Education* (Philadelphia: Lea & Febiger, 1971); John A. Lucas and Ronald A. Smith, *Saga of American Sport* (Philadelphia: Lea & Febiger, 1978); Joan Paul, "The Health Reformers: George Barker Windship and Boston's Strength Seekers," *Journal of Sport History* 10 (Winter, 1983): 41–57; and Scrapbooks I and III.

2. John C. Warren, *Physical Education and the Preservation of Health* (Boston: Ticknor, 1845), pp. 39–41.

3. Catharine Beecher, *Letters to the People on Health and Happiness* (New York: Harper, 1855), pp. 168–171.

4. Mary F. Eastman, *The Biography of Dio Lewis* (New York: Fowler & Wells, 1891).

5. Thomas Wentworth Higginson, "Gymnastics," *Atlantic Monthly* 7 (March 1861): 283–302.

6. School Document No. 15, *Report of the Committee on Physical Training*, June, 1890 (Boston: Rockwell and Churchill, 1890), p. 6.

7. Nils Posse, *Handbook of School Gymnastics of the Swedish System* (Boston: Lee and Shepard, 1891), p. 7.

4: THE STRUGGLE FOR SWEDISH GYMNASTICS IN THE BOSTON SCHOOLS

1. Homans to Armstrong, October 31, 1889, Hampton University Archives, Hampton, VA.

2. Scrapbook III, p. 18.

3. Isabel C. Barrows, ed., *Physical Training* (Boston: George H. Ellis, 1890) pp. 1, 3.

4. Barrows, p. 5.

5. Barrows, p. 20.

6. Barrows, p. 22.

7. Barrows, p. 76.

8. Barrows, p. 79.

9. Barrows, p. 80.

10. Barrows, p. 78.

11. Barrows, p. 96.

12. Barrows, p. 132.

13. "Views on Physical Training," *Boston Herald*, December 1, 1889, p. 8.

14. Barrows, p. 96.

15. *Proceedings of the School Committee of the City of Boston, May, 1889* (Boston: Rockwell and Churchill, 1889), p. 127.

16. School Document No. 10, *1889 Report of the Board of Supervisors on Physical Training in the Public Schools* (Boston: Rockwell and Churchill, 1891), p. 19.

17. "School Committee," *Boston Evening Transcript*, October 9, 1889, p. 11.

18. "Physical Training in Schools," *Boston Post*, November 23, 1889, p. 4.

19. "School Committee," *Boston Evening Transcript*, October 23, 1889, p. 10.

20. "School Committee," *Boston Evening Transcript*, June 25, 1890, p. 10.

5: THE FOUNDING OF THE BOSTON NORMAL SCHOOL OF GYMNASTICS

1. "A Message from Miss Homans," MHAAB, September 1929, p. 3.

2. Fred Eugene Leonard and R. Tait McKenzie, *History of Physical Education* (Philadelphia: Lea & Febiger, 1923), p. 269.

3. William C. King, *Woman* (Springfield, MA: King-Richardson, 1900), p. 490.

4. "A Message from Miss Homans," p. 3.

5. Mary Eloise Talbot '94 in Robinson, p. 9.

6. Talbot in Robinson, pp. 2, 9.

7. CBNSG, 1890–1891, p. 2.

8. "A School of Gymnastics," *Boston Transcript*, January 16, 1889.

9. CBNSG, 1891–1892, p. 8.

10. Report of the President, Massachusetts Institute of Technology, Cambridge, MA, 1893, pp. 19–20.

11. Edith T. Sears '98 in Robinson, p. 7.

12. Register of Graduates, CBNSG, 1891–1892, pp. 15, 16.

6: THE HOMANS TOUCH: EDUCATION OUT OF THE CLASSROOM

1. CBNSG, 1890–1891, p. 5.
2. Charlotte Blatchly McColl '01 in Robinson, p. 7.
3. CBNSG, 1893–1894, p. 17.
4. McColl in Robinson, p. 7.
5. William Shakespeare, *King Lear*.
6. William DeWitt Hyde, Address delivered before the Graduating Class of 1892, DHPE: BNSG, WCA.
7. Charles F. Folsom, Address delivered before the Graduating Class of 1892, DHPE: BNSG, WCA.
8. Kungl. *Gymnastika Centralenstitutet Direktionens Protokoll*, 1889–1891. Vol. A 1:6. National Archives, Stockholm.
9. Homans to the Directors of the R. G. Central Institute, September 1, 1892. Vol. E. 1:12. National Archives, Stockholm.
10. L. M. Törngren, Address delivered before the Graduating Class of 1893, DHPE: BNSG, WCA.
11. MacAlister to Homans, April 13, 1892. Scrapbook I, insert, p. 72.
12. Ethel Perrin, "Ethel Perrin—An Autobiography," in *Pioneer Women in Physical Education, Supplement to the Research Quarterly* 12 (October 1941): 682–685.
13. Homans to Frissell, April 20, 1898, Hampton University Archives, Hampton, VA.
14. Hemenway Papers, Old South Meeting House, Boston, MA.
15. Hemenway Papers, Old South Meeting House.
16. Register of Graduates, CBNSG, 1895–1896, pp. 18–23.

7: FROM GYMNASTIC TEACHERS TO GYMNASUIM DIRECTORS: TOWARD A PROFESSION FOR WOMEN

1. Dudley Allen Sargent, *Health, Strength, and Power*, (New York: Caldwell, 1904), p. 75.
2. CBNSG, 1897–1898, p. 16.
3. CBNSG, 1899–1900, p. 17.
4. CBNSG, 1903–1904, p. 27.
5. CBNSG, 1906–1907, p. 28.
6. CBNSG, 1908–1909, p. 24.
7. CBNSG, 1908–1909, p. 28.
8. CBNSG, 1908–1909, p. 31.
9. CBNSG, 1908–1909, p. 33.
10. CBNSG, 1898–1899, p. 5.
11. See BNSG Catalogues as noted.
12. CBNSG, 1899–1900, p. 16.

13. CBNSG, 1901–1902, pp. 20, 21.

14. Mabel Lee and Bruce L. Bennett, "A Time of Gymnastics and Measurement," *Journal of Health, Physical Education, and Recreation* 31 (April 1960): 26–33.

15. CBNSG, 1908–1909, p. 34.

16. Mabel Lee, *Memories of a Bloomer Girl* (Washington, D.C.: American Alliance for Health, Physical Education, and Recreation, 1977), pp. 101–105.

17. Personal interview with Lucile Grunewald '10, February, 1968.

18. Personal interview with Winifred Van Hagen '04, January, 1968.

19. Personal interview with Marion Mention Hamilton '04, February, 1969.

20. Personal interview with Sarah Davis '07, March, 1968.

21. Personal interview with Fanny Garrison '03, July, 1968.

22. Personal interview with Mary Florence Stratton '00, June, 1968.

23. Personal interview with Winifred Van Hagen '04, January, 1968.

24. Personal interview with Marion Watters Babcock '10, May, 1968.

25. BNSG School Song, Document received from Ruth Elliott '14 and later presented to WCA.

26. American Society for Research in Physical Education (Boston, 1904).

27. "Physical Education," *Mind and Body* 14 (April 1907): 49–50.

28. William James, *Talks to Teachers* (New York: W. W. Norton, 1958), pp. 144, 148.

29. Personal interview with Marion Watters Babcock '10, May, 1968.

30. Clarence J. Blake, "The Spirit of a Profession," pp. 12–15. DHPE: BNSG, WCA.

31. Register of Graduates, CBNSG, 1905–1906, pp. 31–51. In the early years an occasional man enrolled in BNSG. After 1902 the school admitted only women. Seven men are listed in the 1961 *Graduate Register*: Class of 1893—J. Peterson Ryder; 1895—Ernst Hermann, William Skarstrom; 1897—Walter Truslow; 1898—David Holmes; 1899—Clarke Peterson; 1901—Arthur Russell.

8: THE CRISIS IN HOMANS' PLANS

1. Kenneth L. Mark, *Delayed by Fire* (Concord, NH: Rumford, 1945).

2. CBNSG, 1906–1907, p. 54.

3. Minutes of the Corporation of Simmons College, June 11, 1906. The Colonel Miriam E. Perry Goll Archives, Simmons College, Boston, MA.

4. Minutes of the Corporation of Simmons College, January 14, 1907. The Colonel Miriam E. Perry Goll Archives, Simmons College, Boston, MA.

5. BNSG Trustees to Cabot, June 7, 1907, Phillips Library.

6. BNSG Trustees to Homans, March 16, 1907, Phillips Library.

7. "President's Annual Report," *Annual Reports of the President and Treasurer of Wellesley College* (Boston: Wood, 1900), pp. 3–9.

8. BNSG Trustees to Homans, October 30, 1907, Phillips Library.

9. Homans to Frissell, December 3, 1907, and Frissell to Homans, December 27, 1907, Hampton University Archives, Hampton, VA.

10. BNSG Trustees to Homans, November 29, 1907 and February 19, 1908, Phillips Library.

11. A. Hemenway to Homans, March 4, 1908, Phillips Library.

12. CBNSG, 1907–1908, p. 60.

13. Hazard to North, October 7, 1908, ALS File, WCA.

14. Minutes of the Board of Trustees of Wellesley College, June 12, 1908, Wellesley College.

15. Hazard Papers: Mary Hemenway Hall Building Fund, March 30, 1908, WCA.

16. WCB, 1909–1910, pp. 26, 103.

17. CBNSG, 1908–1909, p. 8.

18. CBNSG, 1908–1909, p. 10.

19. Minutes of the Board of Trustees of Wellesley College, February 9, 1906, Wellesley College.

20. Rose L. Donovan, "Lucille Eaton Hill," History: General (1882–1946): Folder II, 3L DHPE, WCA.

21. Ruth C. Hanford, "Lucille Eaton Hill: An Appreciation," *Wellesley Alumnae Magazine* 9 (April 1925): 317, WCA.

22. Hill to Hitchcock, May 22, 1908, Edward Hitchcock '49 Papers, Box 3, Folder 6, Amherst College, Amherst, MA.

23. Amy Morris Homans, "Some Problems in the Administration of a Department of Hygiene in a Woman's College," History: Homans, Amy Morris: Correspondence and Writings (1913–29), 3L DHPE, WCA.

24. WCB, 1909–1910, p. 15.

25. Pendleton to Hazard, February 16, 1909, ALS File, WCA.

26. Pendleton to Hazard, February 16, 1909, ALS File, WCA.

27. BNSG Trustees to Homans, April 9, 1909, Phillips Library.

28. *Who's Who in America*, 1908–09, (Chicago: A. N. Marquis), p. 914.

9: HOMANS AT WELLESLEY: LIBERAL ARTS AND PROFESSIONAL EDUCATION

1. Minutes of the Board of Trustees of Wellesley College, June 12, 1908, and Minutes of the Executive Committee of the Board of Trustees, Wellesley College, August 7, 1908, Wellesley College.

2. Pendleton to Hazard, January 22, 1909, ALS File, WCA.

3. CBNSG, 1908–1909, p. 11.

4. Homans to Hazard, November 15, 1909, ALS File, WCA.

5. Undated newspaper clipping, Mary Hemenway Hall Building Folder, DHPE, WCA.

6. Pendleton to Hazard, December 23, 1908, ALS File, WCA.

7. Pendleton to Hazard, January 22, 1909, ALS File, WCA.

8. "Indoor Meet," *College News*, April 20, 1910, p. 5.

9. See Barbara P. McCarthy, "Traditions," in *Wellesley College, 1875–1975*, ed. Jean Glasscock (Wellesley, MA: Wellesley College, 1975), pp. 235–258.

10. Cocoon: hairstyle of the period.

11. Burr to Spears, undated, History: Spears' Project, 3L DHPE, WCA.

12. Personal interview with Helena Kees '15, May, 1968.

13. Mabel Lee '10, *Memories of a Bloomer Girl*, pp. 172–173.

14. "Edith Hemenway Eustis Memorial Library Fund," DHPE, WCA.

15. Homans to Hazard, July 18, 1910, ALS File, WCA.

16. Wellesley College Annual Reports, 1910, p. 9, WCA.

17. Homans to A. Hemenway, December 15, 1913, History: Homans, Amy Morris: Correspondence and Writings (1913–29), 3L DHPE, WCA.

10: THE WELLESLEY IMAGE IN PHYSICAL EDUCATION FOR WOMEN

1. Homans to A. Hemenway, December 15, 1913, History: Homans, Amy Morris: Correspondence and Writings (1913–29), 3L DHPE, WCA.

2. Howe to Robinson, undated, c. 1914, Howe Folder, DHPE: Faculty File, WCA.

3. WCB, 1911–1912, p. 106.

4. Earle F. Zeigler, "A Brief Descriptive History of Graduate Study in Physical Education in the United States to 1950," in *A History of Physical Education and Sport in the United States and Canada*, ed. Earle F. Zeigler (Chicago: Stipes, 1975), pp. 273–286.

5. Davis to Homans, Report for Year 1914–1915, Department: Annual Reports: Early Courses (1911–1929), 3L DHPE, WCA.

6. WCB, 1917–1918, p. 145.

7. "Notes on a possible new curriculum for the Department of Hygiene" c. 1914, History: General (1882–1946), 3L DHPE, WCA.

8. WCB, 1915–1916, p. 115.

9. MHAAB, 1917–1918, p. 108.

10. "A Message from Miss Homans," MHAAB, September 1929, p. 3.

11. Gorman to Spears, March, 1968.

12. Personal interview with Wilma Haynes '13, March, 1968.

13. Gorman to Spears, March, 1968.

14. Personal interview with Elizabeth Halsey '16, March, 1968.

15. Personal interview with Helen Rockwell '09, March, 1968.

16. Homans to Johnson, undated, possibly May 9, 1910, Archives and Special Collections, Winthrop College, Rock Hill, SC.

17. Homans to Trilling, April 12, 1913, April 15, 1918, and one undated, Archives, Department of Physical Education, University of Wisconsin, Madison, WI.

18. Personal interview with Elizabeth Halsey, March, 1968.

19. MHAAB, 1916–1917, p. 58. (621 represents the number of living; 21 were deceased.)

20. Betty Spears, "Diffusion of a Philosophy," John R. Betts, Address, North American Society for Sport History, May 17-21, 1977.

11: THE PROFESSIONALIZATION OF PHYSICAL EDUCATION FOR WOMEN

1. Mabel Lee and Bruce L. Bennett, "A Time of Athletics and Dancing," *Journal of Health, Physical Education, and Recreation* 31 (April 1960): 38–47.

2. Homans to Pendleton, June 7, 1920, Academic Departments: HPE Folder, President's Office, 1899–1966, WCA.

3. McKinstry to Pratt, May 23, 1915, 7H Alumnae Association: Hygiene and Physical Education, WCA.

4. Pratt to McKinstry, June 12, 1916, and June 14, 1917, 7H Alumnae Association: Hygiene and Physical Education, WCA.

5. Mary Seely Starks '99, "An Appreciation," Annual Report, Mary Hemenway Alumnae Association, 1913–1914, p. 11, 7H Alumnae Association: Hygiene and Physical Education Section, WCA.

6. Marjorie Bouvé '03, Alumni Dinner, Mary Hemenway Alumnae Association, 1914, 7H Alumnae Association: Hygiene and Physical Education Section, WCA.

7. Today the Boston-Bouvé College of Human Development Professions, Northeastern University, Boston, MA.

8. Today the Department of Physical Education, Russell Sage College, Troy, NY.

9. A Report of the Conference Held by the Graduates of the Department of Hygiene and Physical Education at Wellesley College, Wellesley, Massachusetts, June 23 to July 5, 1913, Alumnae Association: Conferences (1913, 1922), 3L DHPE, WCA.

10. "Before 1912," Eastern Association for Physical Education of College Women, The Sophia Smith Collection, Smith College, Northampton, MA.

11. MHAAB, 1918–1919, pp. 6, 7.

12. Minutes of the Executive Committee of the Board of Trustees, June 3, 1918, Wellesley College.

13. MHAAB, 1919–1920, p. 45.

12: STRENGTHENING THE COMMUNITY OF WOMEN PHYSICAL EDUCATORS

1. Homans to Babcock, March 28, 1921.

2. Howe to Robinson, undated, c. 1919–1920. Howe Folder, DHPE: Faculty File, WCA.

3. Personal interview with Helen Edwards Domonkos '22. April, 1968.

4. Homans to the Junior Class on the occasion of her 76th Birthday, 1924, Homans, Amy Morris: Correspondence and Writings (1913–1929), 3L DHPE, WCA.

5. "War Service of Alumnae of Department of Hygiene," War Service: WWI and WWII, 7H Alumnae Association: Hygiene and Physical Education Section, WCA.

6. Homans to Small '18, c. 1924, reported in a personal interview with Mary-Ethel Ball '24, March, 1968.

7. Personal interview with Elizabeth Abbott '24, March, 1968.

8. MHAAB, 1921–1922, p. 75.

9. MHAAB, September 1925, p. 47.

10. MHAAB, September 1925, p. 31.

11. MHAAB, 1924–1925, p. 63.

12. Homans to Alumnae, April 28, 1921, 3L DHPE, WCA.

13. MHAAB, March 1926, p. 39 and Sears to Alumnae, November 10, 1925, Alumni Association: General (1920–60, 1963–4), 3L DHPE, WCA.

14. MHAAB, September 1926, p. 26.

15. Amy Morris Homans, "Some Problems in the Administration of a Department," History: Homans, Amy Morris: Correspondence and Writings (1913–29), 3L DHPE, WCA.

16. Homans to Elliott, undated, c. May, 1930, Facilities and Equipment: Pool Fund Raising, 3L DHPE, WCA.

17. MHAAB, September 1925, p. 32.

18. MHAAB, March 1929, pp. 42, 43.

19. Elliott to Howe, November 30, 1928, and Elliott to McKinstry,

November 30, 1928, History: Homans, Amy Morris: 80th and 85th Birthday Plans (1928–1933), 3L DHPE, WCA.

20. Homans to Garrison, November 30 [1928], and Homans to "My dear friend" [Margaret Johnson], November 19 [1929], History: Homans, Amy Morris: 80th and 85th Birthday Plans (1928–1933), 3L DHPE, WCA.

21. "A Message from Miss Homans," MHAAB, September 1929, pp. 3, 4.

22. Mabel Lee '10, *The Early Years of the American Academy of Physical Education*, 1926–1945, no publisher, 1981.

13: THE FINAL TOUCHES

1. Phyllis Hill, *The Way We Were* (NAPECW, 1975), pp. 7, 8.

2. MHAAB, 1924–1925, p. 43.

3 .Fanny Garrison '03, "Amy Morris Homans—An Appreciation," *The Sportswoman* 5 (February 1929): 8.

4. "Honorary Degree Given Amy Homans," *Boston Globe*, June 9, 1930.

5. *Troy Times*, Troy, NY, June 9, 1930.

6. Lee to Elliott, March 5, 1931, Document received from Ruth Elliott and later presented to WCA.

7. Elliott to Lee, March 10, 1931, Document received from Ruth Elliott and later presented to WCA.

8. Lee to Elliott, May 12, 1931, History: Homans, Amy Morris: 80th and 85th Birthday Plans (1928–1933), 3L DHPE, WCA.

9. MHAAB, 1936–1937, p. 20.

10. American Physical Education Association, "Presentation of Fellowship Awards," *Journal of Health and Physical Education* 2 (June 1931): 14–19. See also Mabel Lee, *Memories Beyond Bloomers* (Washington, D.C.: American Alliance for Health, Physical Education, and Recreation, 1978), pp. 153–155.

11. "Dr. Skarstrom Retires," MHAAB, 1931–1932, p. 8.

12. Homans to Nash, December 20, 1932, Homans Folder, Archives, American Academy of Physical Education, American Alliance for Health, Physical Education, Recreation and Dance, Reston, VA.

13. Personal interview with Marion Watters Babcock '10, May, 1968.

14. Homans to Garrison, June 16, 1933, History: Homans, Amy Morris: 80th and 85th Birthday Plans (1928–1933), 3L DHPE, WCA.

15. MHAAB, 1934–1935, p. 44.

16. Elliott to Dear ———, October 6, 1933, Document received from Ruth Elliott and later presented to WCA.

17. Elliott to McKinstry, October 7, 1933, Document received from Ruth Elliott and later presented to WCA.

18. Elliott to Skarstrom, November 14, 1933, Document received from Ruth Elliott and later presented to WCA.

19. Elliott to Skarstrom, November 14, 1933, Document received from Ruth Elliott and later presented to WCA.

20. Skarstrom to Elliott, October 31, 1933, History: Homans, Amy Morris: Tributes, Obituaries, Biographical Sketches (1933–1935), 3L DHPE, WCA.

21. "Eastern District Association Honors Amy Morris Homans," *The Journal of Health and Physical Education* 5 (June 1934): 28.

22. National Association of Directors of Physical Education for Women in Colleges and Universities, Oberlin College, April 17, 1934, History: Homans, Amy Morris: Tributes, Obituaries, Biographical Sketches (1933–1935), 3L DHPE, WCA.

23. In 1978 the National Association for Physical Education of College Women merged with the National College Physical Education Association for Men to become the National Association for Physical Education in Higher Education.

24. Mabel Lee '10, "Tribute to Amy Morris Homans to Inaugurate the Amy Morris Homans Lectures by the National Association for Physical Education of College Women," The First Amy Morris Homans Lecture, 1967, p. 2.

14: EPILOGUE

1. "A Message from Miss Homans," MHAAB, September 1929, pp. 3, 4.

2. MHAAB, 1917–1918, p. 136.

3. See Chapter 1, pp. 4, 5.

Notes on Sources

The evidence used in this work ranges from widely recognized secondary material on the history of women and the history of physical education to little known primary sources on women's physical education, Mary Hemenway, and Amy Morris Homans. In this brief essay it is impossible to mention all the books, periodicals, and papers consulted; however, some of the more helpful materials are cited and may be useful to those who wish to pursue these topics.

The literature on the history of women in the United States has increased markedly since the research for this book began. Sources for general information on the history of women in the United States in the latter half of the nineteenth century include *The Woman in America*, edited by Robert Jay Lifton (Boston, 1964), William L. O'Neill's *Everyone Was Brave* (Chicago, 1969), Eleanor Flexner's *Century of Struggle* (Cambridge, 1959), and Page Smith's *Daughters of the Promised Land* (Boston, 1970). Additional background material can be found in June Sochen's *Movers and Shakers* (New York, 1973), *Root of Bitterness*, the collection edited by Nancy F. Cott (New York, 1972), and Barbara Welter's *Dimity Convictions* (Athens, 1976). Many other books, chapters in books, and articles in journals such as *Signs* contain pertinent material.

The standard work on the history of women in education is Thomas Woody's *A History of Women's Education in the United States* (New York, 1929). It provides an extensive account of women's education during the period of this study. Mabel Newcomer's *A Century of Higher Education for Women* (New York, 1959) details the prejudices faced by proponents of higher education for women in the nineteenth century. Excellent collections on the history of women's education may be found in the Margaret Clapp Library at Wellesley College, Wellesley, MA and the Sophia Smith Collection, Smith College, Northampton, MA. E. H.

Clarke's *Sex in Education* (Boston, 1873) is in both collections. Bibliographies and footnotes in many of these secondary works refer to valuable primary sources in earlier articles and documents.

Works such as Arthur M. Schlesinger's *The Rise of the City* (New York, 1933) furnish a general understanding of the many changes which occurred in American cities in the late-nineteenth century. Elisabeth M. Herlihy's *Fifty Years of Boston* (Boston, 1932) offers a detailed picture of Boston at the turn of the century and also refers to the Hemenway family. Other helpful sources on Boston include Arthur Mann's *Yankee Reformers in the Urban Age* (Cambridge, 1954) and Barbara M. Solomon's *Ancestors and Immigrants* (Cambridge, 1956). The official *Proceedings of the School Committee of the City of Boston*, the annual reports of the School Committee, and School Documents (Boston, 1883–1890) detail the actions by the committee and the role played by Hemenway and Homans in introducing gymnastics to the Boston public schools.

In the beginning of the research, materials on Mary Hemenway and Amy Morris Homans appeared elusive, but, gradually, the necessary evidence was found in places ranging from Salem, MA to Wilmington, NC. Brief biographical sketches of Mary Hemenway appear in the *Cyclopaedia of American Biographies* and the *Dictionary of American Biography*. Frederic A. Eustis' biography of Augustus Hemenway, Mary Hemenway's husband, (Salem, MA, 1955) led to the Phillips Library of the Peabody Museum at Salem. A wealth of Hemenway family papers is housed there. These helped locate further Hemenway information in the basement of Boston's Old South Meeting House, a closet in the Boston Athenaeum, and the Widener and Andover-Harvard Theological Libraries at Harvard University. Together with Katherine H. Stone's article "Mrs. Mary Hemenway and Household Arts in the Boston Public Schools" (*The Journal of Home Economics*, January, 1929), these papers document Hemenway's philanthropic endeavors in Boston, Wilmington, and other Southern cities. The reports of the Soldiers' Memorial Society (Boston, 1866–1868) establish the connection of Amy Morris Bradley to the Reconstruction projects in Wilmington. The Edward Everett Hale papers at the Andover-Harvard Theological Library contain letters from Bradley describing the Wilmington schools and the difficulties experienced by the Northern teachers.

Two genealogies, Lucy Ann Carhart's *Genealogy of the Morris Family* (New York, 1911) and *Memoranda of the Descendents of Amos Morris of East Haven, Conn.* (New York, 1853) trace the Homans family to the early settlers in New England. An interview with Homans' niece, Hope Homans Clark, added helpful details about Homans' family background. Nineteenth century education at Oak Grove Seminary is fully described in Raymond R. Manson and Elsia Holway Burleigh's *First Seventy Years of Oak Grove Seminary* (Vassalboro, ME, 1965). William Skarstrom's biography of Homans in *Pioneer Women in Physical Education, Supplement to the Research Quarterly* (October, 1941) did not agree with evidence found on Amy Morris Bradley and in Wilmington. Reports of Bradley's work appear in Frances E. Willard and Mary C. Livermore's *American Women* (New York, 1897) and Julia Ward Howe's *Sketches of Representative Women of New England* (Boston, 1904).

The account presented in this book is based on a careful study of Bradley's life, Bradley's correspondence located at the Andover-Harvard Theological Library, and primary sources found at the Board of Education in Wilmington. Charles Lowe's article on Bradley's schools (*Old and New*, June, 1870) provides helpful material. Walter L. Fleming's *Documentary History of Reconstruction* (Cleveland, 1907), Henry Lee Swint's *The Northern Teacher in the South: 1862–1870* (New York, 1967), and local accounts housed in the Wilmington library contain important background data on Southern education during Reconstruction and Homans' years in the South. Newspaper accounts, especially in the Hemenway papers in the Boston Athenaeum, supply information on Homans' activities after she joined Hemenway in Boston.

While the importance of the 1889 Conference in the Interest of Physical Training is generally recognized by historians of physical education, most authors treat the Boston Normal School of Gymnastics briefly as part of the beginnings of teacher training in physical education. Until recently, scant attention was given to the history of women's physical education. For this work, sources of the period proved to be more helpful. Edward M. Hartwell's *Physical Training in American Colleges and Universities* (Washington, 1886) is used in this work as evidence of physical education during the late-nineteenth century. The publication of the 1889 conference proceedings (Isabel C. Barrows, *Physical Training*, Boston, 1890) is the basis for the chapter on "The Struggle for Swedish Gymnastics in the Boston Schools."

Fred E. Leonard's *History of Physical Education*, edited by R. Tait McKenzie (Philadelphia, 1923), provides a detailed account of the introduction of gymnastics to the United States. Leonard also includes material on the Royal Central Institute of Gymnastics in Stockholm and Per Henrik Ling, the founder of Swedish gymnastics. Additional information on the relationship between the Boston Normal School of Gymnastics and the Royal Central Institute of Gymnastics is housed in the National Archives in Stockholm. The *American Physical Education Review* (1886–1929) and *Mind and Body* (1894–1936) contain a number of articles dealing with women's physical education. Ellen W. Gerber's

Innovators and Institutions in Physical Education (Philadelphia, 1971) brings a more recent perspective to Leonard and McKenzie's work and furnishes additional data.

Two recent books address the history of women's physical education and sport more fully. John A. Lucas and Ronald A. Smith's *Saga of American Sport* (Philadelphia, 1978) treats women topically, while Betty Spears and Richard A. Swanson interweave the history of women's physical education and sport throughout their work, *History of Sport and Physical Activity in the United States* (Dubuque, IA, 1983). Other sources on the history of women in physical education and sport are *The American Woman in Sport*, Ellen W. Gerber, Jan Felshin, Pearl Berlin, and Waneen Wyrick, (Reading, MA, 1974), Stephanie L. Twin's *Out of the Bleachers* (New York, 1979), and Reet Howell's anthology, *Her Story in Sport*, (West Point, NY, 1982). Research by Spears, especially "Influences on Early Professional Physical Education Curriculums in the United States", (Second Canadian Symposium on the History of Sport and Physical Education, 1972), "The Emergence of Women in Sport," (*Women's Athletics: Coping with Controversy*, Washington, 1974), and "The Diffusion of a Philosophy," (North American Society of Sport History, 1977) adds original material to this work. Recent articles on the history of women in physical education and sport can be found in *Quest*, the *Journal of Sport History*, and the *Canadian Journal of History of Sport*.

In spite of the fact that Homans had many of her papers destroyed, documents from the Boston Normal School of Gymnastics and Wellesley College provided information for major portions of this book. These records are housed in the Wellesley College Archives. The Hemenway scrapbooks (I, 1889–1893; II, 1900–1903; and III, 1889–1894), largely a collection of newspaper clippings and articles, are invaluable. Other scrapbooks include accounts of school functions, invitations to social events, and other memorabilia of life at the Boston Normal School of Gymnastics. Carefully preserved files contain accounts of department meetings, copies of commencement addresses, student papers, announcements of professional meetings, and records of alumnae activities. The Boston Normal School of Gymnastics *Catalogues* give data on the administration of the school, course offerings, alumnae placement, and other details.

Information relative to the affiliation of the Boston Normal School of Gymnastics with Wellesley College can be found in the Phillips Library, the Minutes of the Executive Committee of the Board of Trustees of Wellesley College, the Minutes of the Board of Trustees of Wellesley College, and the papers of Caroline Hazard and Ellen Fitz Pendleton in the Wellesley College Archives. The Wellesley College *Bulletin*, the *College News*, and department files provide sources on faculty, curriculum, and student activities during the Wellesley period. The Mary Hemenway Alumnae Association *Bulletins* (1916–1937) contain information about the department and alumnae functions. They also give valuable information on women's physical education of the period. Ruth Elliott's correspondence provides the basis for the account of Homans' financial situation during the last years of her life.

The personal recollections of the alumnae of both the Boston Normal School of Gymnastics and Wellesley College have made this work possible. The material found in the document prepared by Elmo A. Robinson is most helpful. The alumnae who permitted me to interview them and who often sent letters relating incidents and describing Amy Morris Homans deserve to be mentioned:

Boston Normal School of Gymnastics: Class of 1899—Elizabeth Berenson; 1900—Mary Florence Stratton; 1903—Fanny Garrison; 1904—Marion Luey Johnson, Marion Mention Hamilton, Winifred Van Hagen; 1907—Eleanor Davis Ehrman, Sarah Davis; 1908—Ethel Manchester; 1909—Helen Rockwell; 1909-1910, Charlotte Rey Burr.

Wellesley College: Class of 1910—Lucile Grunewald, Mabel Lee, Marion Watters Babcock; 1911—Helen Blake Goddard, Anna Hughitt; 1913—Wilma Haynes, Gertrude Manchester; 1914—Violet Marshall; 1915—Gertrude Baker, Jo Guion Hunt, Helena Kees, Marion Lyon Schwob; 1916—Louise Cobb, Gladys Gorman, Elizabeth Halsey, Mary McKee; 1917—Eline von Borries, Katharine Hersey Oberteuffer; 1918—Eleanor Bartlett, Marie Carns; 1919—Louisa May Greeley, Helen Hazelton, Marie Henze Glass; 1922—Helen Edwards Domonkos, Josephine Rathbone Karpovich; 1922-1923—Gladys Bassett; 1924—Elizabeth Abbott, Mary-Ethel Ball, Bessie Rudd; 1926—Anna Espenschade.

Index

About the Author

BETTY SPEARS, Professor Emerita of Physical Education, University of Massachusetts at Amherst, is the author of *History of Sport and Physical Activity in the United States* and several other books, and has contributed chapters to others. Her articles have appeared in such diverse journals as the *New England Quarterly*, the *Journal of Sport History*, *National Forum*, and *Quest*.

Recent Titles in
Contributions in Women's Studies